Sam P. Jones

Great Awakening

a choice collection of new and standard gospel songs

Sam P. Jones

Great Awakening
a choice collection of new and standard gospel songs

ISBN/EAN: 9783337265724

Printed in Europe, USA, Canada, Australia, Japan

Cover: Foto ©Lupo / pixelio.de

More available books at **www.hansebooks.com**

THE GREAT AWAKENING,

A CHOICE COLLECTION OF NEW AND STANDARD

GOSPEL SONGS,

PREPARED UNDER THE PERSONAL SUPERVISION OF

REV. SAM. P. JONES,

FOR USE IN ALL

GOSPEL MEETINGS.

THE GREAT AWAKENING,

A CHOICE COLLECTION OF NEW AND STANDARD

GOSPEL SONGS,

PREPARED UNDER THE PERSONAL SUPERVISION OF

REV. SAM. P. JONES,

FOR USE IN ALL

GOSPEL MEETINGS.

CINCINNATI:

Published by The JOHN CHURCH CO., 74 W. Fourth St.

CHICAGO:
Root & Sons Music Co.
200 Wabash Ave.

NEW YORK:
The J. Church Co.
55 E. 13th St.

May be ordered of Booksellers and Music Dealers.

PREFACE.

"THE GREAT AWAKENING" is brimming full of the poetry and melodies especially adapted to wide-awake Christian work and workers. Each song, both new and old, has passed under my eye. My Musical Director, Mr. M. J. Maxwell, has helped me glean from all the fields of song already in print, and many new pieces will be found in this book by the best known authors, which were prepared especially for this work. Many good standard hymns have also been added, to make the book practical for all services.

I shall use this book in preference to all others, wherever my work shall engage me, because I believe it is the best book of songs in existence, and as such I commend it heartily to all who want sentiment and music in harmony with the best Christian thought and the most enlightened methods.

Sam. P. Jones

CARTERSVILLE, GEORGIA, *April* 15, 1886.

Copyright, 1886, by THE JOHN CHURCH CO.

The Great Awakening.

No. 1.   Happy Day.   L. M.

1. { Oh, happy day, that fixed my choice On Thee, my Savior and my God;
    Well may this glowing heart rejoice, And tell its raptures all a-broad. }

CHORUS.

Hap-py day, hap-py day, When Je-sus washed my sins a - way!
D. S. Hap-py day, hap-py day, When Je-sus washed my sins a - way!

He taught me how to watch and pray, And live re-joic-ing ev-'ry day;

2 Oh, happy bond that seals my vows
   To Him who merits all my love!
Let cheerful anthems fill His house,
   While to that sacred shrine I move.

3 'Tis done, the great transaction's done!
   I am my Lord's, and He is mine;
He called me, and I followed on,
   Charmed to confess the voice divine.

4 Now rest, my long divided heart!
   Fixed on this blissful center, rest;
Here have I found a noble part,
   Here heavenly pleasures fill my breast.

5 High heaven that heard the solemn vow,
   That now renewed shall daily hear;
Till in life's latest hour I bow,
   And bless in death a bond so dear.

No. 2. "Whosoever Will."

"Whosoever will, let him take the water of life freely."—Rev. 22: 17.

P. P. Bliss. P. P. Bliss, by per.

Joyfully.

1. "Who-so-ev-er heareth," shout, shout the sound! Send the blessed tidings all the world around; Spread the joyful news wherev-er man is found:
2. Who-so-ev-er com-eth, need not de-lay, Now the door is o-pen, en-ter while you may; Je-sus is the true, the on-ly Liv-ing Way:
3. "Who-so-ev-er will," the promise se-cure; "Who-so-ev-er will," for-ev-er must en-dure; "Whosoev-er will," 'tis life for ev-er-more:

CHORUS.

"Who-so-ev-er will, may come." "Who-so-ev-er will, who-so-ev-er will," Send the proc-la-ma-tion o-ver vale and hill; 'Tis a lov-ing Fa-ther calls the wand'rer home: "Who-so-ev-er will, may come."

No. 3.   **Call Them In.**

E. O. E.   E. O. Excell.

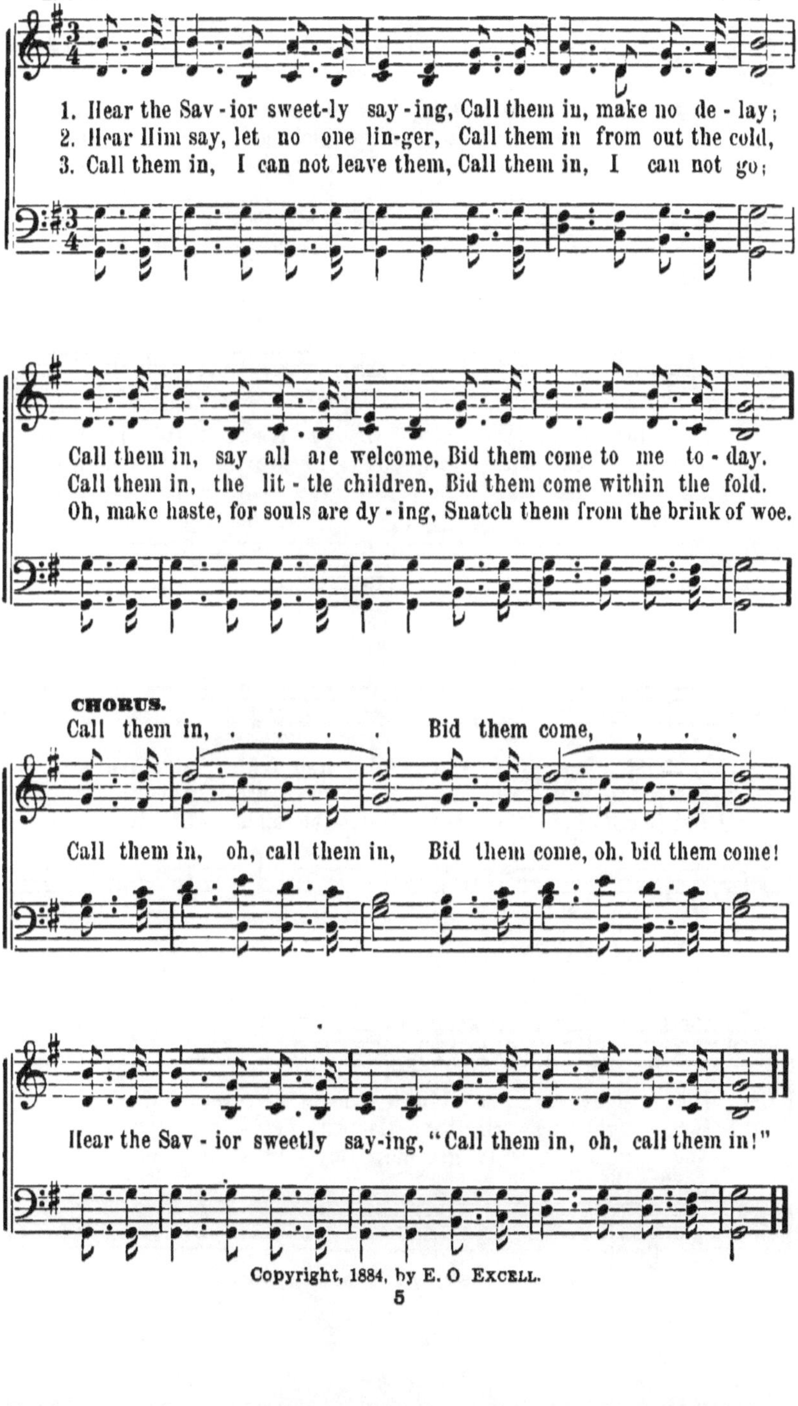

1. Hear the Sav-ior sweet-ly say-ing, Call them in, make no de-lay;
2. Hear Him say, let no one lin-ger, Call them in from out the cold,
3. Call them in, I can not leave them, Call them in, I can not go;

Call them in, say all are welcome, Bid them come to me to-day.
Call them in, the lit-tle children, Bid them come within the fold.
Oh, make haste, for souls are dy-ing, Snatch them from the brink of woe.

CHORUS.
Call them in, ... Bid them come, . . .
Call them in, oh, call them in, Bid them come, oh, bid them come!

Hear the Sav-ior sweetly say-ing, "Call them in, oh, call them in!"

Copyright, 1884, by E. O Excell.

The Crown of Glory. Concluded.

4 The foes that assail me stand forth in their pride,
Within and around me on every side;
But armed and equipped by my King, I am strong,
And know that, in battle, I'll vanquish the wrong.
  For a crown, for a crown, for a crown I fight,
  With Christ as my leader, my strength and my light.

5 God's battle will win at the last, I am sure,
Though long the great conflict with sin may endure,
His power, and justice and love will unite,
To brighten the earth with the triumphs of right.
  For a crown, for a crown, for a crown I fight,
  With Christ as my leader, my strength and my light.

The Light of the World is Jesus. Concluded.

Once I was blind, but now I can see; The Light of the world is Je-sus.

No. 6. What Hast Thou Done for Me?

"So Christ was once offered to bear the sins of many."—HEB. 9: 28.

Miss FRANCES R. HAVERGAL.   P. P. BLISS, by per.

Moderato.

1. I gave my life for thee, My pre-cious blood I shed,
2. My Fa-ther's house of light,— My glo-ry-cir-cled throne,

That thou might'st ransomed be, And quickened from the dead;
I left for earth-ly night, For wand'rings sad and lone;

I gave, I gave My life for thee, What hast thou given for Me?
I left, I left it all for thee, Hast thou left aught for Me?

3 I suffered much for thee,
  More than thy tongue can tell,
Of bitterest agony,
  To rescue thee from hell;
I've borne, I've borne it all for thee,
What hast thou borne for me?

4 And I have brought to thee,
  Down from my home above,
Salvation full and free,
  My pardon and My love;
I bring, I bring rich gifts to thee,
What hast thou brought to Me?

No. 7. Shall I be Saved To-night?

"Look unto me, and be ye saved."—ISAIAH 45:22.

FANNY J. CROSBY.   Mrs. M. BLISS WILSON, by per.

1. Je-sus is pleading with my poor soul, Shall I be saved to-night?
2. Je-sus was nailed to the cross for me, Shall I be saved to-night?
3. Je-sus is knocking at my poor heart, Shall I be saved to-night?
4. What if that voice I should hear no more, Shall I be saved to-night?

If I be-lieve, He will make me whole, Shall I be saved to-night?
How can my heart so un-grate-ful be? Shall I be saved to-night?
What if His spir-it should now de-part? Shall I be saved to-night?
Quick-ly I'll o-pen this bolt-ed door, Save me, O Lord, to-night.

Ten-der-ly, sad-ly I hear Him say, How can you grieve me from day to day?
Now He will save me by grace divine, Now, if I will, I may call him mine;
O-ver and o-ver His voice I hear, Sweetly it falls on my list'ning ear;
Blessed Redeemer, come in, come in, Pit-y my sorrow, for-give my sin;

Shall I go on in the old, old way, Or shall I be saved to-night?
Can I the pleasures of earth re-sign? Oh, shall I be saved to-night?
Shall I re-ject Him—a friend so dear? Oh, shall I be saved to-night?
Now let Thy work in my soul be-gin, For I will be saved to-night?

No. 10.   **Beautiful Land on High.**

J. NICHOLSON.   C. A. HAVENS, by per.

1. There's a beau-ti-ful land on high, To its glo-ries I fain would fly; When by
2. There's a beau-ti-ful land on high, I shall en-ter it by and by; There with

sorrows pressed down, I long for my crown, In that beautiful land on high.
friends hand in hand, I'll walk on the strand, In that beautiful land on high.

CHORUS.

In that beau-ti-ful land I'll be, ... From earth and its cares set free; ...
                       I'll be,   set free;

My Je-sus is there, He's gone to prepare A place in that land for me, for me.

3 There's a beautiful land on high,
Then why should I fear to die?
When death is the way to the realms
    of the day
In that beautiful land on high.

There's a beautiful land on high,
And my kindred its bliss enjoy;
Me-thinks I now see how they're
    waiting for me
In that beautiful land on high.

Copyright, 1886, by THE JOHN CHURCH CO.

No. 11. Are you Washed in the Blood?

Words and Music by Rev. ELISHA A. HOFFMAN.

1. Have you been to Jesus for the cleansing pow'r? Are you washed in the blood of the Lamb? Are you fully trusting in his grace this hour? Are you washed in the blood of the Lamb?
2. Are you walk-ing dai-ly by the Savior's side? Are you washed in the blood of the Lamb? Do you rest each moment in the Cru-ci-fied? Are you washed in the blood of the Lamb?
3. When the Bridegroom cometh, will your robes be white, Pure and white in the blood of the Lamb? Will your soul be ready for the mansions bright, And be washed in the blood of the Lamb?
4. Lay aside the garments that are stained with sin, And be washed in the blood of the Lamb? There's a fountain flowing for the soul unclean, Oh, be washed in the blood of the Lamb?

CHORUS.

Are you washed in the blood, In the soul-cleansing blood of the Lamb? Are your garments spotless? Are they white as snow? Are you washed in the blood of the Lamb?

Copyright, E. A. HOFFMAN.

No. 13. Are You Ready?

MARY D. JAMES.   JNO. R. SWENEY, by per.

1. Should the summons, quickly fly-ing, On the slumb'ring nations fall,— Lo! the Heav'nly Bridegroom cometh, Would the sound your souls ap-pall?

CHORUS.
Are you ready? Are you ready? Should you hear the midnight call?
Are you ready? Are you ready? Should you hear the midnight call?
Are you ready? Are you ready? Should you hear the midnight call? Should you hear the mid-night call?

2 What if now the startling mandate
  Should the sleeping virgins hear,—
Are your lamps all trimmed and burning
  Should the Bridegroom now appear?
|: Are you ready? Are you ready?
  Now to see your Lord appear? :|

3 Is there oil in all your vessels?
  Are your garments pure and white?
Are they washed in the cleansing Fountain,
  Fit to stand in Jesus' sight?
|: Are you ready? Are you ready?
  Are your lamps all clear and bright? :|

4 Rise! ye virgins,—sleep no longer,—
  Lest the call your souls surprise!
Lest ye fail to meet the Bridegroom,
  When He cometh from the skies.
|: Oh, be ready! Oh, be ready!
  Hasten, from your slumbers rise! :|

No. 14. Welcome for Me.

FANNY J. CROSBY.   WM. J. KIRKPATRICK, by per.

1. Like a bird on the deep, far a-way from its nest, I had wander'd, my Sav-ior, from Thee; But Thy dear lov-ing voice call'd me home to Thy breast, And I knew there was wel-come for me.
2. I am safe in the ark; I have fold-ed my wings On the bo-som of mer-cy di-vine; I am fill'd with the light of Thy pres-ence so bright, And the joy that will ev-er be mine.
3. I am safe in the ark, and I dread not the storm, Tho' a-round me the sur-ges may roll; I will look to the skies, where the day nev-er dies, I will sing of the joy in my soul.

CHORUS.

Wel-come for me, Sav-ior, from Thee; A smile and a welcome for me: Now, like a dove, I rest in Thy love, And find a sweet refuge in Thee, in Thee.

From "SONGS OF JOY."

No. 15. Precious Promise.

"Whereby are given unto us exceeding great and precious promises."—2 Pet. 1:4.

NATHANIEL NILES.   P. P. BLISS, by per.

1. Precious promise God hath giv-en To the wea-ry pass-er by,
2. When temptations al-most win thee, And thy trusted watchers fly,
3. When thy secret hopes have perished, In the grave of years gone by,
4. When the shades of life are fall-ing, And the hour has come to die,

On the way from earth to heaven, "I will guide thee with Mine eye."
Let this promise ring within thee, "I will guide thee with Mine eye."
Let this promise still be cherished, "I will guide thee with Mine eye."
Hear thy trusty Pi-lot call-ing, "I will guide thee with Mine eye."

REFRAIN.

I will guide thee, I will guide thee, I will guide thee with Mine eye;

On the way from earth to heaven, I will guide thee with Mine eye.

No. 16. Redemption's Story.

J. R. M.
J. R. MURRAY.

1. Let us sing redemption's sto-ry, Let us sing the Sav-ior's love,
2. Praise, oh, praise the love that sought us While we walked in wicked ways;
3. With His mighty arms around us, We can nev-er faint or fear;

Sons of God and heirs of glo-ry, Praise Him till ye meet a-bove!
Praise, oh, praise the love that bought us, Give it ev-er-last-ing praise.
In His keep-ing who has found us, All the way is bright and clear.

CHORUS.

Let us sing redemption's sto-ry, Sing a-loud the sweet re-frain,

Till the an-gel hosts in glo-ry Send the ech-o back a-gain.

Copyright, 1886, by THE JOHN CHURCH CO.

No. 17. When Jesus Comes.

"Unto them that look for him shall he appear the second time, without sin, unto salvation."—HEB. 9: 28.

P. P. BLISS.   P. P. BLISS, by per.

1. Down life's dark vale we wander, Till Jesus comes; We watch and
2. Oh, let my lamp be burning, When Jesus comes; For Him my
3. No more heart-pangs nor sadness, When Jesus comes; All peace and
4. All doubts and fears will vanish, When Jesus comes; All gloom His

wait and won-der, Till Jesus comes.
soul be yearn-ing, When Jesus comes.
joy and glad-ness, When Jesus comes.
face will ban-ish, When Jesus comes,

CHORUS.

All joy His loved ones bringing, When Jesus comes; All praise thro' heaven ringing, When Jesus comes. All beauty bright and vernal, When Jesus comes; All glory, grand, eternal, When Jesus comes.

When Jesus Comes. Concluded.

5 He'll know the way was dreary,
  When Jesus comes;
  He'll know the feet grew weary,
  When Jesus comes.—Cho.

6 He'll know what griefs oppressed me,
  When Jesus comes;
  Oh, how His arms will rest me!
  When Jesus comes.—Cho.

No. 18. The Sure Foundation.

T. C. O'KANE, by per.

1. There stands a Rock, on shores of time, That rears to heav'n its head sublime, That Rock is cleft, and they are blest, Who find with-in the cleft a rest. Some build their hopes on the ev-er drifting sand, Some on their fame, or their treasure, or their land, Mine's on a Rock that forever will stand, Je-sus the "Rock of Ag-es."

2 That Rock's a cross, its arms outspread,
  Celestial glory bathes its head;
  To its firm base my all I bring,
  And to the cross of ages cling.

3 That Rock's a tower whose lofty height,
  Illumed with heaven's unclouded light,
  Opes wide its gates beneath the dome,
  Where saints find rest with Christ at home.

My Redeemer. Concluded.

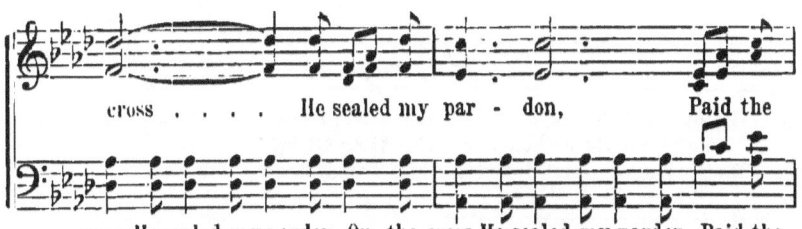

cross .... He sealed my par-don, Paid the
cross He sealed my pardon, On the cross He sealed my pardon, Paid the

Repeat *pp* after last verse.

debt, ... and made me free, and made me free.
debt, and made me free,

No. 20. Dennis. S. M.

Rev. JOHN FAWCETT, 1772. From H. G. NAGELI.

1. Blest be the tie that binds Our hearts in Christian love;
2. Be-fore our Fa-ther's throne, We pour our ar-dent prayers;
3. We share our mu-tual woes; Our mu-tual bur-dens bear;
4. When we a-sun-der part, It gives us in-ward pain:

The fel-low-ship of kin-dred minds Is like to that a-bove.
Our fears, our hopes, our aims are one,—Our com-forts and our cares.
And oft-en for each oth-er flows The sym-pa-thiz-ing tear.
But we shall still be joined in heart, And hope to meet a-gain.

No. 22.   **Almost Persuaded.**

"Almost thou persuadest me to be a Christian."—ACTS 26: 28.

P. P. BLISS, by per.

1. "Almost persuaded" now to believe;
"Almost persuaded" Christ to receive.
Seems now some soul to say, "Go, Spirit, go thy way,
Some more convenient day On thee I'll call."

2. "Almost persuaded," come, come today;
"Almost persuaded," turn not away.
Jesus invites you here, Angels are ling'ring near,
Prayers rise from hearts so dear; O wand'rer come!

3. "Almost persuaded," harvest is past;
"Almost persuaded," doom comes at last.
"Almost" can not avail; "Almost is but to fail!
Sad, sad that bitter wail—"Almost, but lost!"

No. 23. Hear the Call.

"Put on the whole armor of God."—Eph. 6: 11.

W. F. S.   W. F. Sherwin, 1879, by per.

March movement.

1. Lo! the day of God is breaking; See the gleaming from a-far!
2. Trust in Him who is your Captain; Let no heart in ter-ror quail;
3. Onward marching, firm and steady, Faint not, fear not Satan's frown,
4. Conq'ring hosts with banners waving, Sweeping on o'er hill and plain,

Sons of earth from slumber waking, Hail the bright and Morning Star.
Je-sus leads the gath'ring le-gions, In His name we shall pre-vail.
For the Lord is with you al-ways, Till you wear the Victor's crown.
Ne'er shall halt till swells the anthem, "Christ o'er all the world shall reign!"

CHORUS.

Hear the call! O gird your armor on, Grasp the Spirit's mighty Sword:
Take the hel-met of sal-va-tion, Pressing on to battle for the Lord!

No. 24. Glorious Fountain.

W. COWPER. T. C. O'KANE, by per.

1. There is a fountain filled with blood, filled with blood, filled with blood,
And sinners plunged beneath that flood, beneath that flood, beneath that flood,
2. The dy-ing thief re-joiced to see, re-joiced to see, re-joiced to see,
And there may I, tho' vile as he, tho' vile as he, tho' vile as he.

There is a fountain filled with blood, Drawn from Immanuel's veins,
And sinners plunged beneath that flood, Lose all their guilt-y stains.
The dy-ing thief rejoiced to see That fountain in his day,
And there may I, tho' vile as he, Wash all my sins a-way.

CHORUS.

Oh, glo-ri-ous fount-ain! Here will I stay,
And in thee ev-er Wash my sins a-way.

3 Thou dying Lamb, |: Thy precious blood :|
Shall never lose its power,
Till all the ransomed |: Church of God :|
Are saved, to sin no more.

4 E'er since by faith |: I saw the stream :|
Thy flowing wounds supply,
Redeeming love |: has been my theme, :|
And shall be till I die.

Copyright 1881, by T. C. O'KANE.

No. 26. **Who Cares for a Soul?**

J. B. O. CLEMM.

1. Who cares for a soul? say, Christian, do you? Or will you, with empty hand, Meet the Master and say there is nothing to do, When He your accounts shall demand.
2. Who'll speak to that soul that hastens apace To death and eternal woe? Who will tell it of Jesus in accents of love, And point out the way it should go.
3. Who of us that cares when called to account, To hear from the King, "Well done," And to see mid the shining ones gathered around, Some souls that our labors have won.

REFRAIN.
Who cares? .... Who cares? ... Who cares for a soul to-day? Then haste to the wand'rers and make no delay, And beg them to come to the fold.
Cares for a soul, Cares for a soul?

Copyright, 1886, by THE JOHN CHURCH Co.

No. 27. Draw me Nearer.

"Let us draw near with a true heart."—HEB. 10: 22.

FANNY J. CROSBY.   W. H. DOANE, by per.

1. I am Thine, O Lord, I have heard Thy voice, And it told Thy love to me;
2. Consecrate me now to Thy service, Lord, By Thy pow'r of grace divine;

But I long to rise in the arms of faith, And be closer drawn to Thee.
Let my soul look up with a steadfast hope, And my will be lost in Thine.

CHORUS.

Draw me near-er, nearer, blessed Lord, To the cross where Thou hast died;
nearer, nearer,

Draw me nearer, nearer, nearer, blessed Lord, To Thy precious, bleeding side.

3 O the pure delight of a single hour
   That before Thy throne I spend,
When I kneel in pray'r, and with Thee,
   my God,
   I commune as friend with friend.

4 There are depths of love that I can
   not know
   Till I cross the narrow sea,
There are heights of joy that I may not
   reach
   Till I rest in peace with Thee.

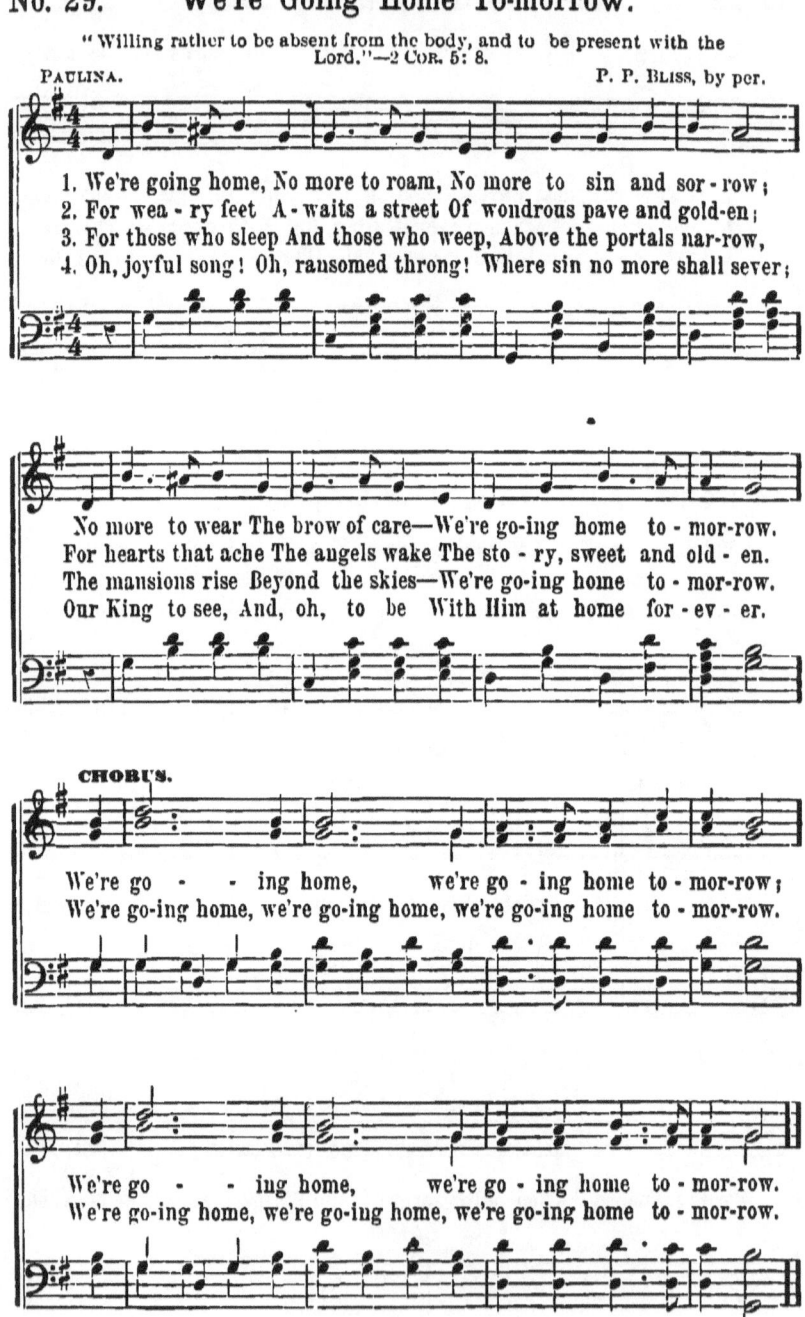

No. 31. Trusting in the Promise.

"He is faithful that promised."—HEB. 10: 23.

Rev. H. B. HARTZLER.   Rev. E. S. LORENZ.

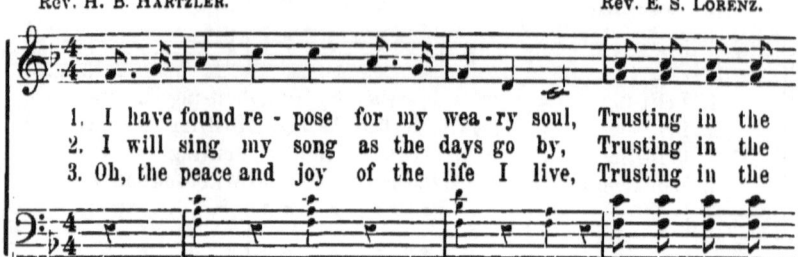

1. I have found re - pose for my wea - ry soul, Trusting in the
2. I will sing my song as the days go by, Trusting in the
3. Oh, the peace and joy of the life I live, Trusting in the

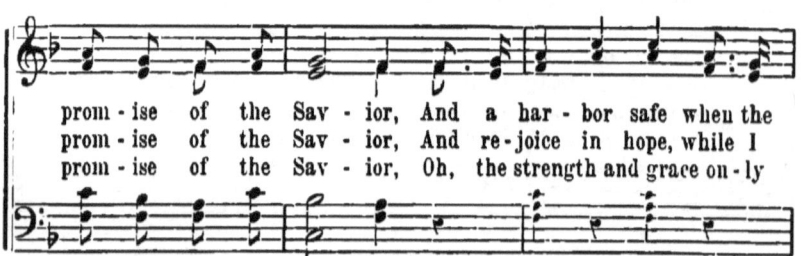

prom - ise of the Sav - ior, And a har - bor safe when the
prom - ise of the Sav - ior, And re - joice in hope, while I
prom - ise of the Sav - ior, Oh, the strength and grace on - ly

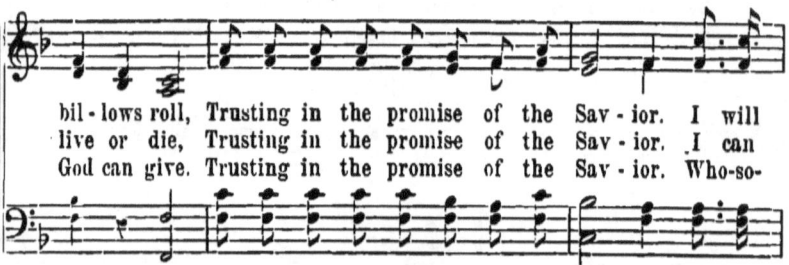

bil - lows roll, Trusting in the promise of the Sav - ior. I will
live or die, Trusting in the promise of the Sav - ior. I can
God can give. Trusting in the promise of the Sav - ior. Who-so-

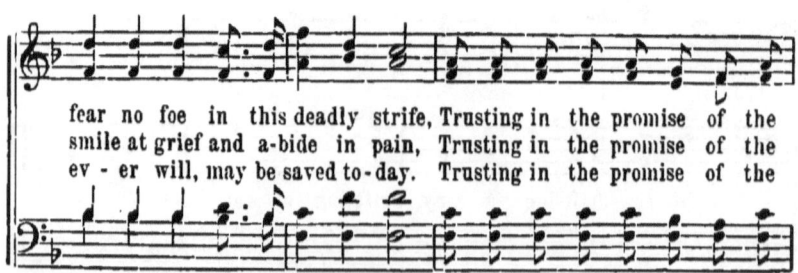

fear no foe in this deadly strife, Trusting in the promise of the
smile at grief and a-bide in pain, Trusting in the promise of the
ev - er will, may be saved to-day. Trusting in the promise of the

Copyright, 1878, by E. S. LORENZ. By per.

Trusting in the Promise. Concluded.

Sav - ior; I will bear my lot in the toil of life, Trusting in the
Sav - ior; And the loss of all shall be highest gain, Trusting in the
Sav - ior; And be-gin to walk in the ho - ly way, Trusting in the

REFRAIN.

prom - ise of the Sav - ior. Rest-ing on His mighty arm for-ev - er, Nev - er from His lov - ing heart to sev - er, I will rest by grace In His strong embrace, Trusting in the promise of the Sav-ior.

No. 32.　　Gloria Patri.　　ANON.

Glory be to the Father, and to the Son, and to the Ho - ly Ghost.
As it was in the beginning, is now, and . . . . ev - er shall be, world with-out end. A - men.

No. 33. Welcome to Glory.

PHŒBE PALMER.   Mrs. JOSEPH F. KNAPP, by per.

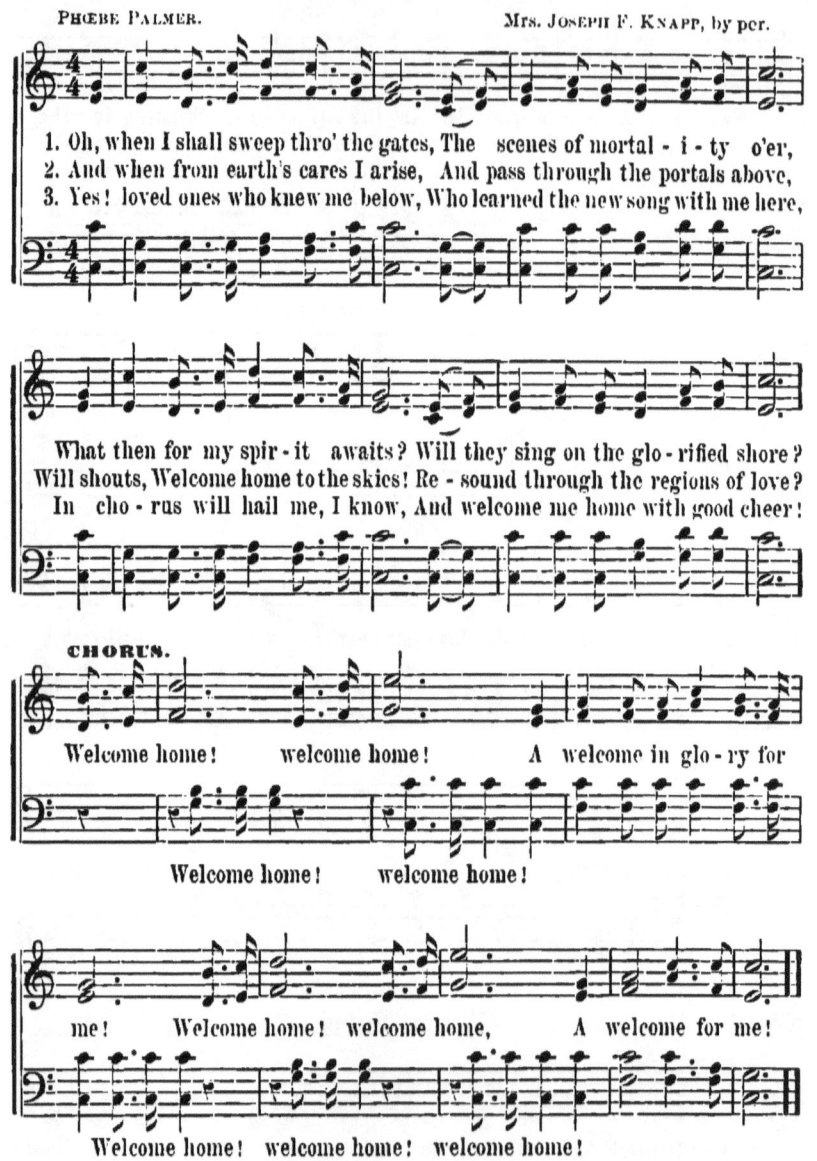

1. Oh, when I shall sweep thro' the gates, The scenes of mortal-i-ty o'er,
2. And when from earth's cares I arise, And pass through the portals above,
3. Yes! loved ones who knew me below, Who learned the new song with me here,

What then for my spir-it awaits? Will they sing on the glo-rified shore?
Will shouts, Welcome home to the skies! Re-sound through the regions of love?
In cho-rus will hail me, I know, And welcome me home with good cheer!

CHORUS.

Welcome home! welcome home! A welcome in glo-ry for me! Welcome home! welcome home, A welcome for me!

4 The beautiful gates will unfold,
   The home of the blood-washed I'll see;
The city of saints I'll behold!
   For, oh! there's a welcome for me!

5 A sinner made whiter than snow,
   I'll join in the mighty acclaim,
And shout through the gates as I go,
   Salvation to God and the Lamb!

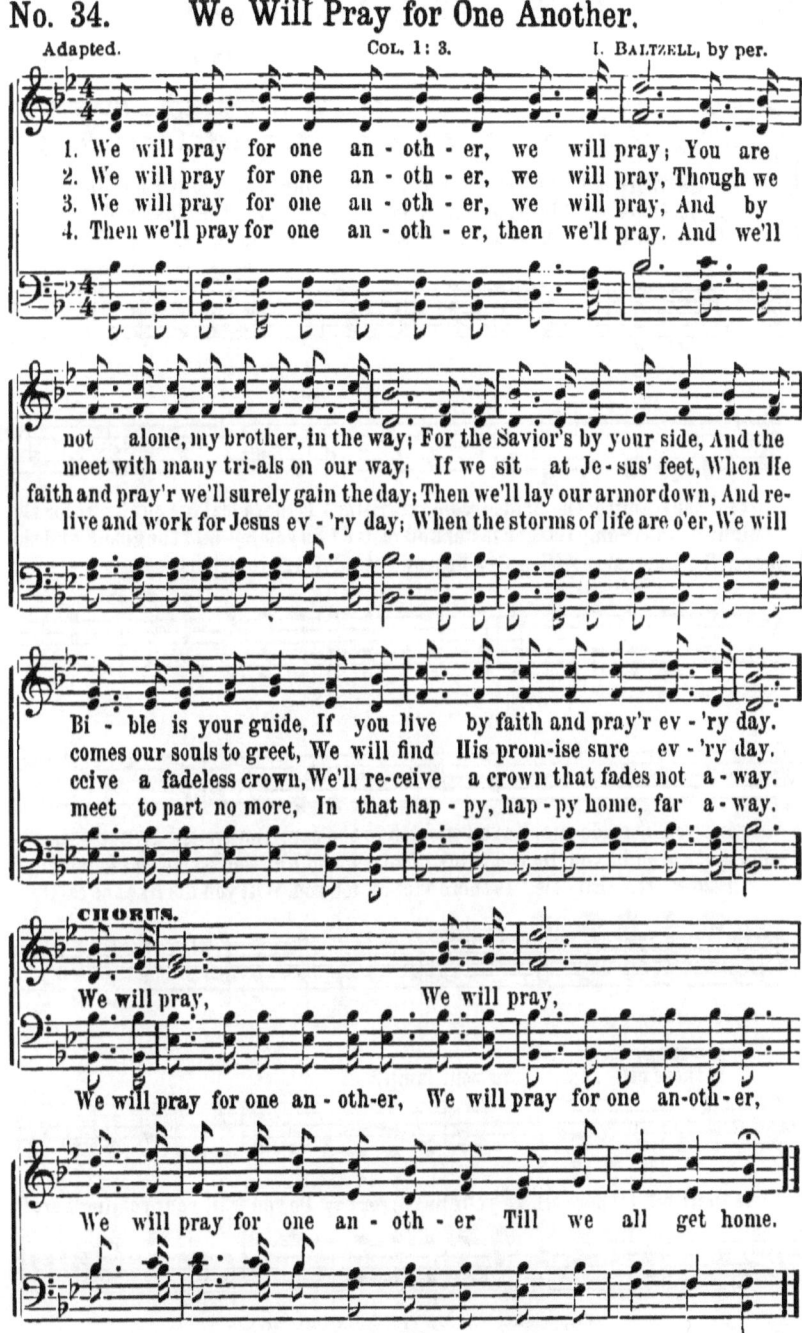

No. 35. Is There Oil in Your Lamp?

T. P. W.
Thos. P. Westendorf.

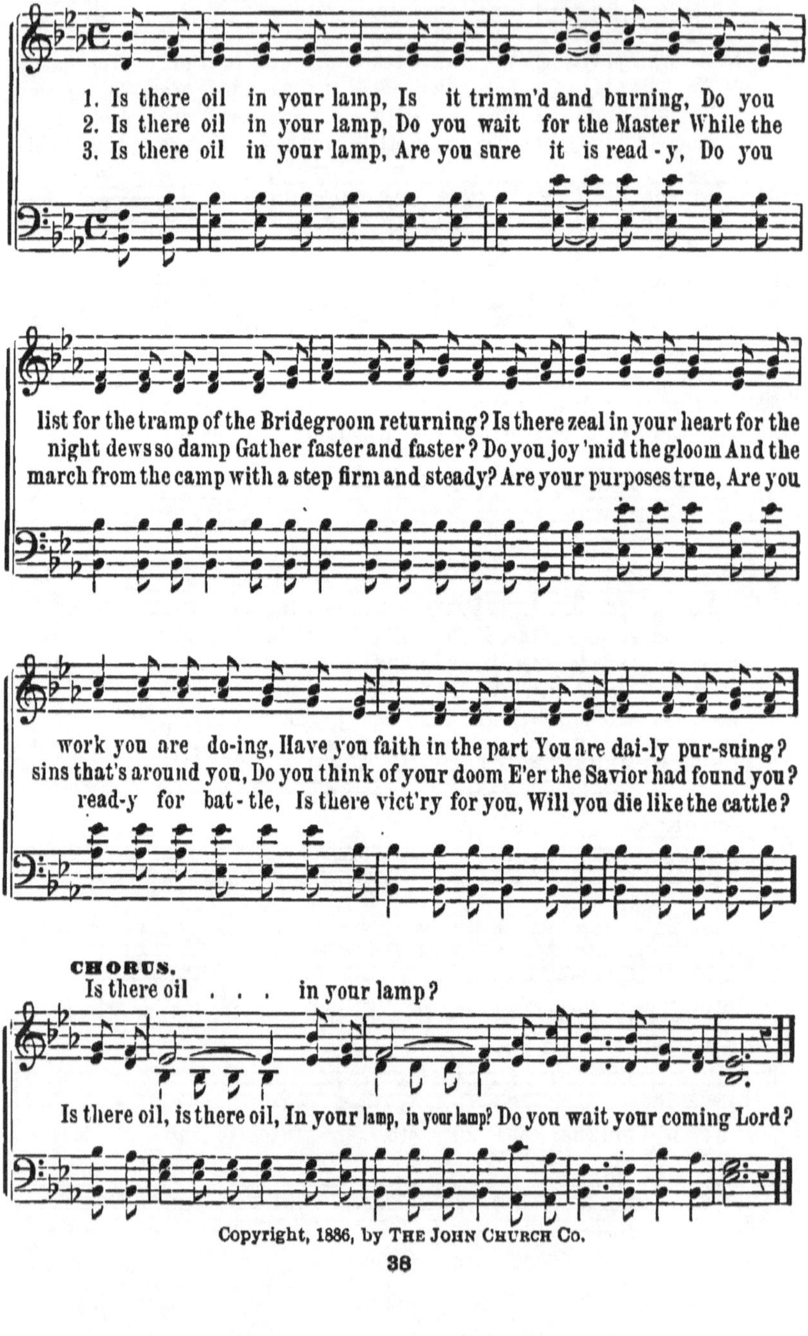

1. Is there oil in your lamp, Is it trimm'd and burning, Do you
2. Is there oil in your lamp, Do you wait for the Master While the
3. Is there oil in your lamp, Are you sure it is read-y, Do you

list for the tramp of the Bridegroom returning? Is there zeal in your heart for the
night dews so damp Gather faster and faster? Do you joy 'mid the gloom And the
march from the camp with a step firm and steady? Are your purposes true, Are you

work you are do-ing, Have you faith in the part You are dai-ly pur-suing?
sins that's around you, Do you think of your doom E'er the Savior had found you?
read-y for bat-tle, Is there vict'ry for you, Will you die like the cattle?

CHORUS.
Is there oil . . . in your lamp?

Is there oil, is there oil, In your lamp, in your lamp? Do you wait your coming Lord?

Copyright, 1886, by The John Church Co.

No. 36. Our Glad Jubilee.

W. F. SHERWIN. WM. F. SHERWIN, by per.

D. C. Wake, wake the song! etc.

1. Wake, wake the song! our glad ju-bi-lee Once more we hail with sweet mel-o-dy, Bringing our hymn of praise unto Thee, Oh, most holy Lord! Praise for Thy care by day and by night, Praise for the homes by love made so bright; Thanks for the pure and soul-cheering light Beaming from Thy word.

2. March-ing to Zi-on, dear blessed home! Lord, by thy mer-cy hither we come; Guide us we pray where'er we may roam, Keep us in Thy fear; Fill every soul with love all divine, Now cause Thy face upon us to shine; Grant that our hearts may tru-ly be Thine All the com-ing year. Then

3. Yet once a-gain the an-them re-peat, Join ev-ery voice the Master to greet; Love's sac-ri-fice we lay at His feet, In His temple now; Je-sus, accept the off'ring we bring, Blending with songs the odors of spring; Still of Thy wondrous love we will sing Till in heaven we bow.

That Old, Old Story is True. Concluded.

No. 38. God be with You.

Rev. J. E. RANKIN. W. G. TOMER, by per.

1. God be with you till we meet again; By His counsels, guide, uphold you,
2. God be with you till we meet again, 'Neath His wings securely hide you;

With His sheep securely fold you, God be with you till we meet again.
Dai-ly man-na still di-vide you, God be with you till we meet again.

CHORUS.

Till we meet,... till we meet, Till we meet at Jesus' feet;
Till we meet, till we meet again, till we meet;

Till we meet,... till we meet, God be with you till we meet again.
Till we meet, till we meet again.

3 God be with you till we meet again,
  When life's perils thick confound you;
  Put his arms unfailing round you,
God be with you till we meet again.

4 God be with you till we meet again,
  Keep love's banner floating o'er you;
  Smite death's threatening wave before you,
  God be with you till we meet again.

No. 39. **Sound the Battle-cry.**

Wm. F. Sherwin. Wm. F. Sherwin, by per.

1. Sound the bat-tle-cry! See! the foe is nigh; Raise the standard high
2. Strong to meet the foe, Marching on we go, While our cause we know,
3. Oh! Thou God of all, Hear us when we call, Help us one and all

For the Lord; Gird your ar-mor on, Stand firm ev-ery one; Rest your
Must pre-vail; Shield and banner bright Gleaming in the light; Battling
By Thy grace; When the battle's done, And the vict'ry won, May we

CHORUS. *ff*

cause up-on His ho-ly word.
for the right We ne'er can fail. Rouse, then, soldiers, rally round the banner,
wear the crown Before Thy face.

Read-y, stead-y, pass the word a-long; On-ward, for-ward,

shout a-loud Ho-san-na! Christ is Cap-tain of the mighty throng.

No. 40. Rescue the Perishing.

"Go out into the highways and hedges, and compel them to come in, that my house may be filled."—LUKE 14: 23.

FANNY J. CROSBY.   W. H. DOANE, by per.

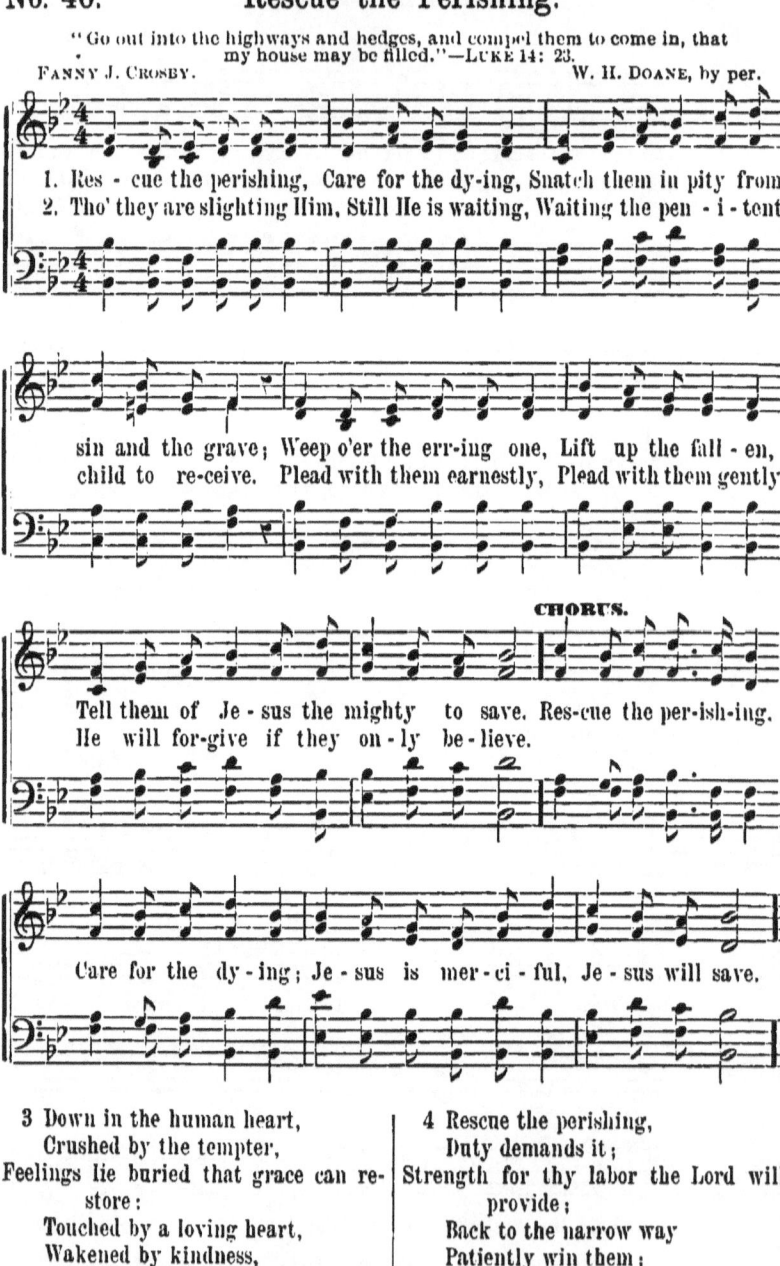

3 Down in the human heart,
  Crushed by the tempter,
Feelings lie buried that grace can restore:
  Touched by a loving heart,
  Wakened by kindness,
Chords that were broken will vibrate once more.

4 Rescue the perishing,
  Duty demands it;
Strength for thy labor the Lord will provide;
  Back to the narrow way
  Patiently win them;
Tell the poor wanderer a Savior has died.

More to Follow. Concluded.

Oh, His matchless, boundless love, Still there's more to fol-low.

No. 43.   Lenox.   6s & 8s.

Rev. Ch. Wesley, 1749.   J. Edson, 1782.

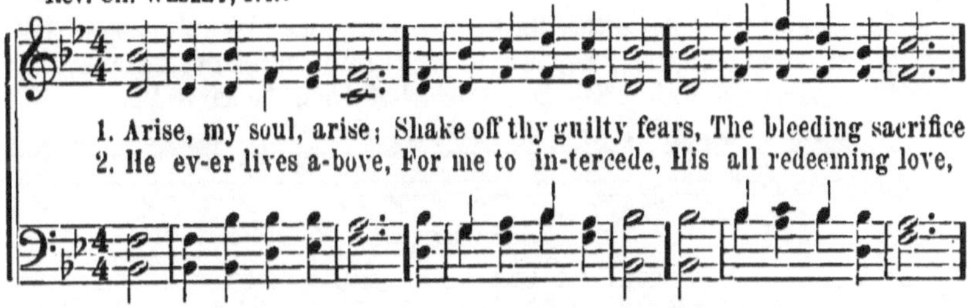

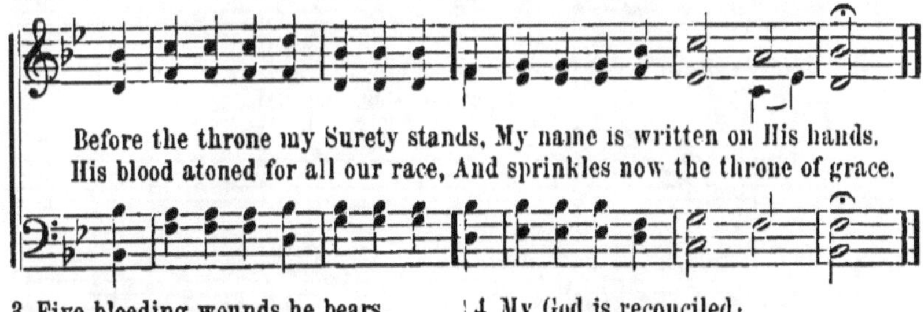

1. Arise, my soul, arise; Shake off thy guilty fears, The bleeding sacrifice
2. He ev-er lives a-bove, For me to in-tercede, His all redeeming love,

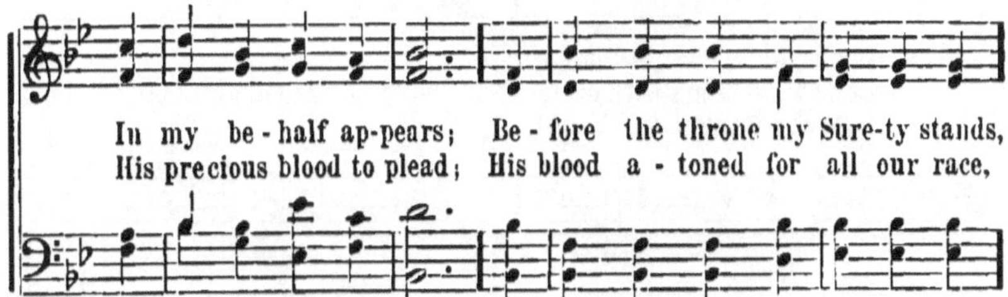

In my be-half ap-pears; Be-fore the throne my Sure-ty stands,
His precious blood to plead; His blood a-toned for all our race,

Before the throne my Surety stands, My name is written on His hands.
His blood atoned for all our race, And sprinkles now the throne of grace.

3 Five bleeding wounds he bears,
   Received on Calvary;
  They pour effectual prayers,
   They strongly plead for me;
Forgive him, oh, forgive, they cry,
Nor let that ransomed sinner die.

4 My God is reconciled;
   His pardoning voice I hear;
  He owns me for His child;
   I can no longer fear;
With confidence I now draw nigh,
And Father, Abba, Father, cry.

No. 48. Pull for the Shore.

"Therefore, if any man be in Christ, he is a new creature; old things are passed away, behold, all things are become NEW."—2 Cor. 5: 17.

"Therefore, my beloved . . . work out your own salvation with fear and trembling." —Phil. 2: 12.

P. P. Bliss. P. P. Bliss, by per.

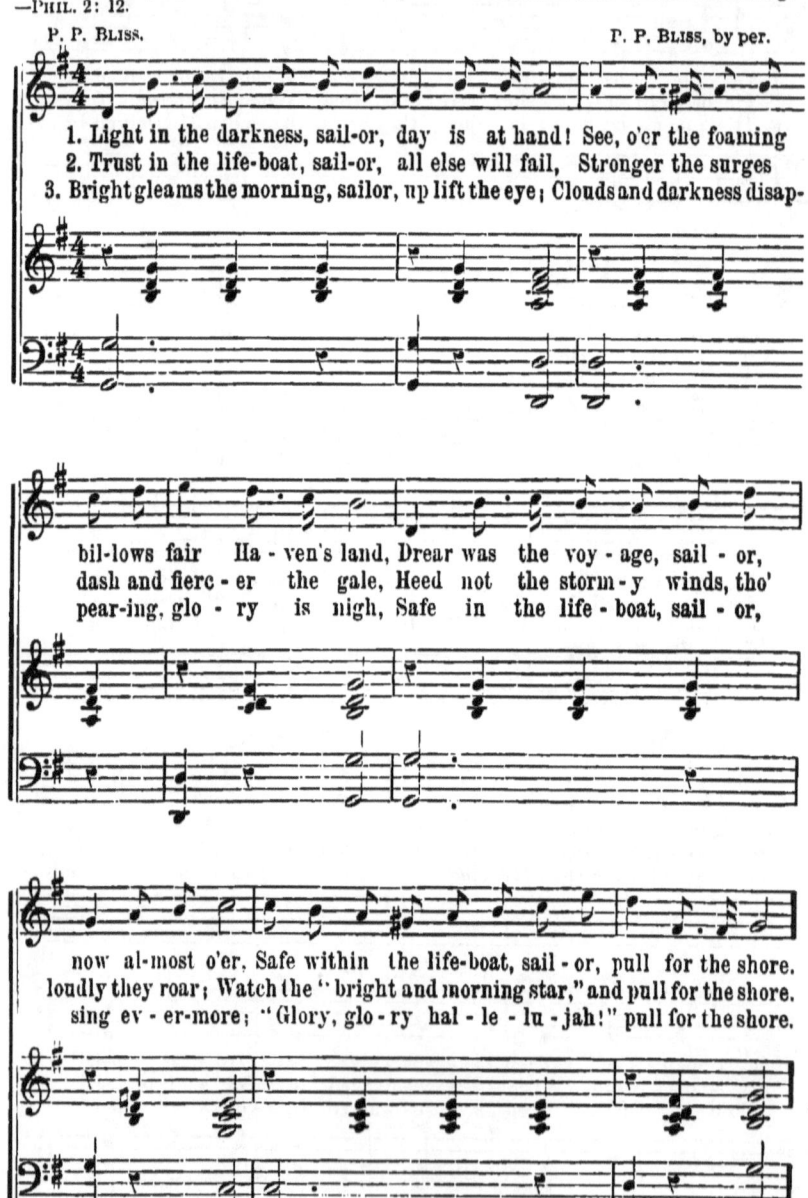

1. Light in the darkness, sail-or, day is at hand! See, o'er the foaming billows fair Haven's land, Drear was the voyage, sailor, now almost o'er, Safe within the life-boat, sailor, pull for the shore.

2. Trust in the life-boat, sail-or, all else will fail, Stronger the surges dash and fiercer the gale, Heed not the stormy winds, tho' loudly they roar; Watch the "bright and morning star," and pull for the shore.

3. Bright gleams the morning, sailor, uplift the eye; Clouds and darkness disappearing, glory is nigh, Safe in the life-boat, sailor, sing evermore; "Glory, glory hallelujah!" pull for the shore.

Pull for the Shore. Concluded.

O Prodigal, Don't Stay Away. Concluded.

There's a kiss, kind and true; Then, O prod-i-gal, don't stay a-way.

No. 50.   Marcellus. 7s.

M. J. MAXWELL.

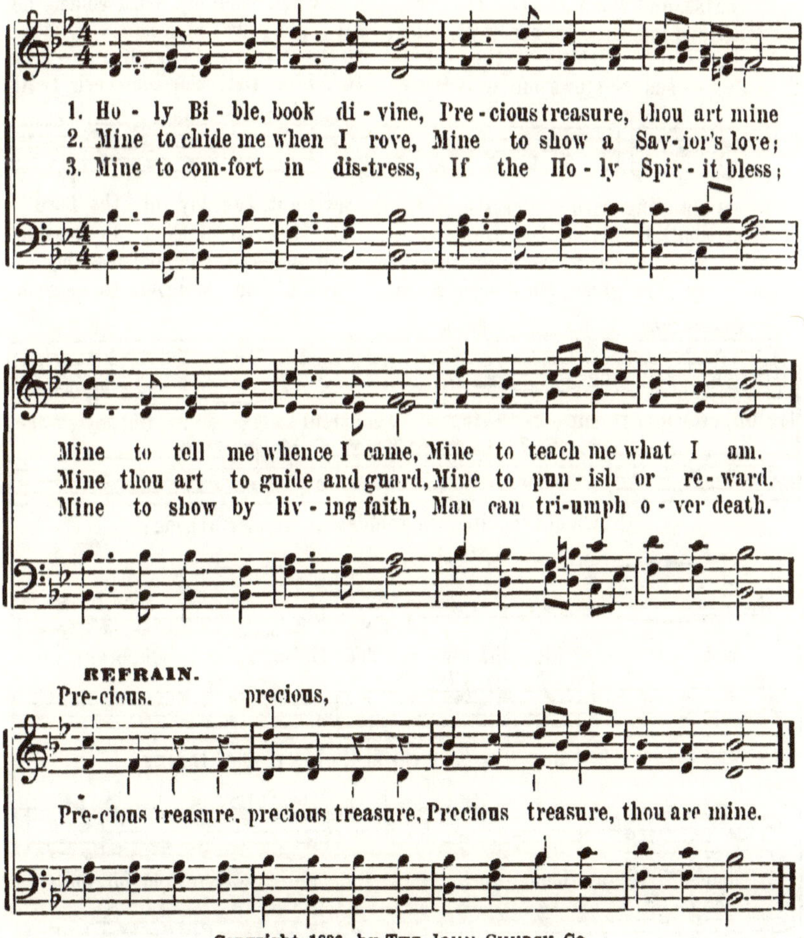

1. Ho-ly Bi-ble, book di-vine, Pre-cious treasure, thou art mine
2. Mine to chide me when I rove, Mine to show a Sav-ior's love;
3. Mine to com-fort in dis-tress, If the Ho-ly Spir-it bless;

Mine to tell me whence I came, Mine to teach me what I am.
Mine thou art to guide and guard, Mine to pun-ish or re-ward.
Mine to show by liv-ing faith, Man can tri-umph o-ver death.

REFRAIN.

Pre-cious, precious,

Pre-cious treasure, precious treasure, Precious treasure, thou are mine.

Copyright, 1886, by THE JOHN CHURCH CO.

No. 51 Oh, Crown of Rejoicing.

"Henceforth there is laid up for me a crown of righteousness."—2 Tim. 4: 8.

Rev. J. B. Atkinson.   P. P. Bliss, by per.

DUET.

1. Oh, crown of re-joic-ing that's waiting for me, When finished my
2. Oh, won-der-ful song that in glo-ry I'll sing, To Him who re-
3. Oh, joy ev-er-last-ing when heav-en is won, For-ev-er in
4. Oh, won-der-ful name which the glo-ri-fied bear, The new name which

course, and when Je-sus I see, And when from my Lord comes the
deemed me, to Je-sus my King; All glo-ry and hon-or to
glo-ry to shine as the sun; No sor-row or sigh-ing—these
Je-sus be-stows on us there; To him that o'er-com-eth 'twill

sweet sounding word: "Receive, faithful serv-ant, the joy of thy Lord."
Him shall be given, And prais-es un-ceas-ing for-ev-er in heaven.
all flee a-way, No night there, no shad-ows—'tis one end-less day.
on-ly be given, Blest sign of ap-prov-al, our welcome to heaven.

CHORUS.

Oh, crown of re-joic - ing, Oh, wonderful song; . . Oh, joy ev-er-
Crown of rejoicing, Oh, wonderful, wonderful song;

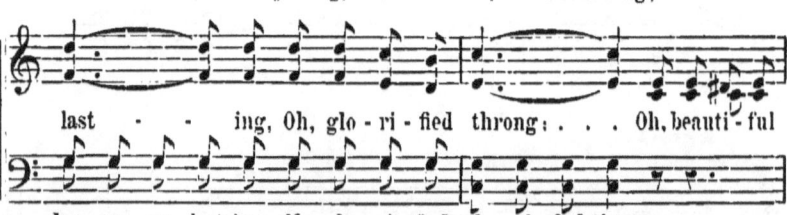

last - - ing, Oh, glo - ri - fied throng; . . . Oh, beauti - ful
Joy ev - er - last-ing, Oh, glo - ri - fied, glo - ri - fied throng;

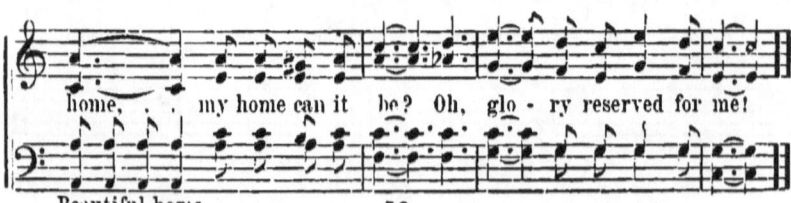

home, . . my home can it be? Oh, glo - ry reserved for me!
Beautiful home,

No. 52. When the King Comes in.

J. E. LANDOR. Rev. E. S. LORENZ, by per.

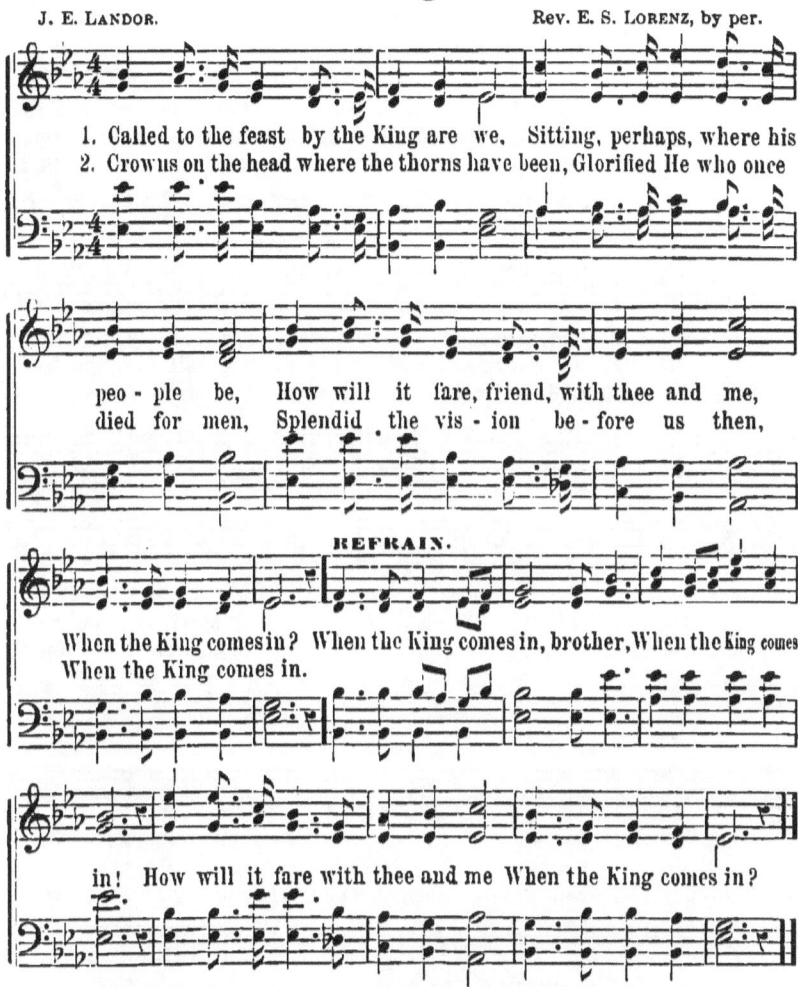

1. Called to the feast by the King are we, Sitting, perhaps, where his peo-ple be, How will it fare, friend, with thee and me,
2. Crowns on the head where the thorns have been, Glorified He who once died for men, Splendid the vis-ion be-fore us then,

REFRAIN.

When the King comes in? When the King comes in, brother, When the King comes in! How will it fare with thee and me When the King comes in?
When the King comes in.

3 Like lightning's flash will that in-
  stant show
Things hidden long from both friend
  and foe,
Just what we are will each neighbor
  know,
When the King comes in.

4 Joyful shall his eye on each one rest
Who is in white wedding garments
  dressed,

Ah, well for us if we stand the test
When the King comes in.

5 Endless the separation then,
Bitter the cry of deluded men,
Awful that moment beyond all ken,
When the King comes in.

6 Lord, grant us all, we implore Thee,
  grace,
So to await thee each in his place,
That we may fear not to see Thy face
When Thou comest in.

Copyright, 1879, by E. S. LORENZ.

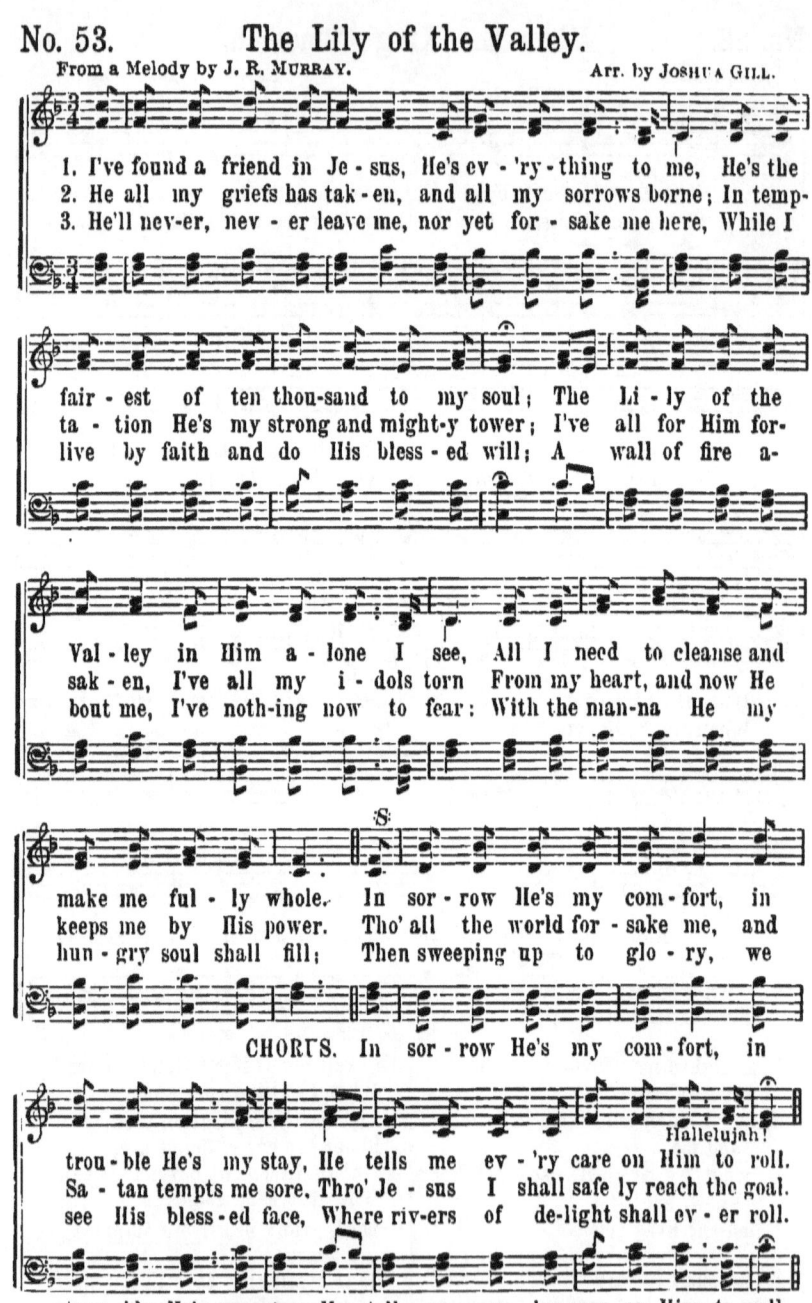

The Lily of the Valley. Concluded.

He's the Li-ly of the Val-ley, the bright and morn-ing
He's the Li-ly of the Val-ley, the bright and morn-ing
Star, He's the fair-est of ten thou-sand to my soul.
Star, He's the fair-est of ten thou-sand to my soul.

No. 54. It is Good to be Here.

Rev. ISAAC N. WILSON.   JNO. R. SWENEY, by per.

1. While we bow in Thy name, oh, meet us a-gain; Fill our
   hearts with the light of Thy love.
   May the Spir-it of grace, and the smiles of Thy face, Gent-ly
   fall on us now from a-bove. It is good to be here, It is
   good for us, Lord, to be here.
   good to be here; Thy perfect love now drives a-way all our fear, And
   light streaming down makes the pathway all clear: It is

2 Our souls long for Thee; Oh, may we now see
  A sin-cleansing blood-wave appear;
  And feel as it rolls in power o'er our souls,
  It is good for us, Lord, to be here.

3 Thou art with us, we know; we feel the sweet flow
  Of the sin-cleansing wave's gladd'ning tide;
  We are washed from our sin, made all holy within,
  And in Jesus we sweetly abide.

Copyright, 1879, by JNO. R. SWENEY.

No. 55. **The Ninety and Nine.**

P. P. BLISS, by per.

2 Shepherd, hast Thou not here Thy ninety and nine ;
Are they not enough for Thee ?
But the Shepherd replied, "This one of mine.
Has wandered away from me ;
The way may be wild and rough and steep.
I go to the desert to find my sheep."

3 But none of the ransomed ever knew
How deep were the waters crossed,
Nor how dark was the night the Lord passed through

Ere He found the sheep that was lost.
Away in the desert He heard its cry,
So feeble and helpless and ready to die.

4 And afar up the mountain, thunder riven,
And along the rocky steep,
There arose the glad song of joy to heaven,
"Rejoice, I have found my sheep!"
And the angels echoed around the throne,
"Rejoice, for the Lord brings back His own!"

No. 56. Clinging Close to Jesus.

ELIZA M. SHERMAN.   J. R. MURRAY.

1. Are you clinging, clinging close to Je-sus With the steadfast hand of love? Treading ev-er, ev-er in His foot-steps, To the heav'nly home a-bove.
2. Do you trust Him, trust Him on the mountain, As upon thy Gal-i-lee? Knowing, know-ing that what-e'er He send-eth Sure-ly is the best for thee.
3. Art thou clinging, clinging close to Je-sus? In His home thou shalt a-bide; Thou shalt see Him, see Him in His glo-ry, There thou shalt be sat-is-fied.

CHORUS.

Clinging close to Je-sus, Clinging to His hand; He will sure-ly lead you To the prom-ised land.

Copyright, 1886, by THE JOHN CHURCH Co.

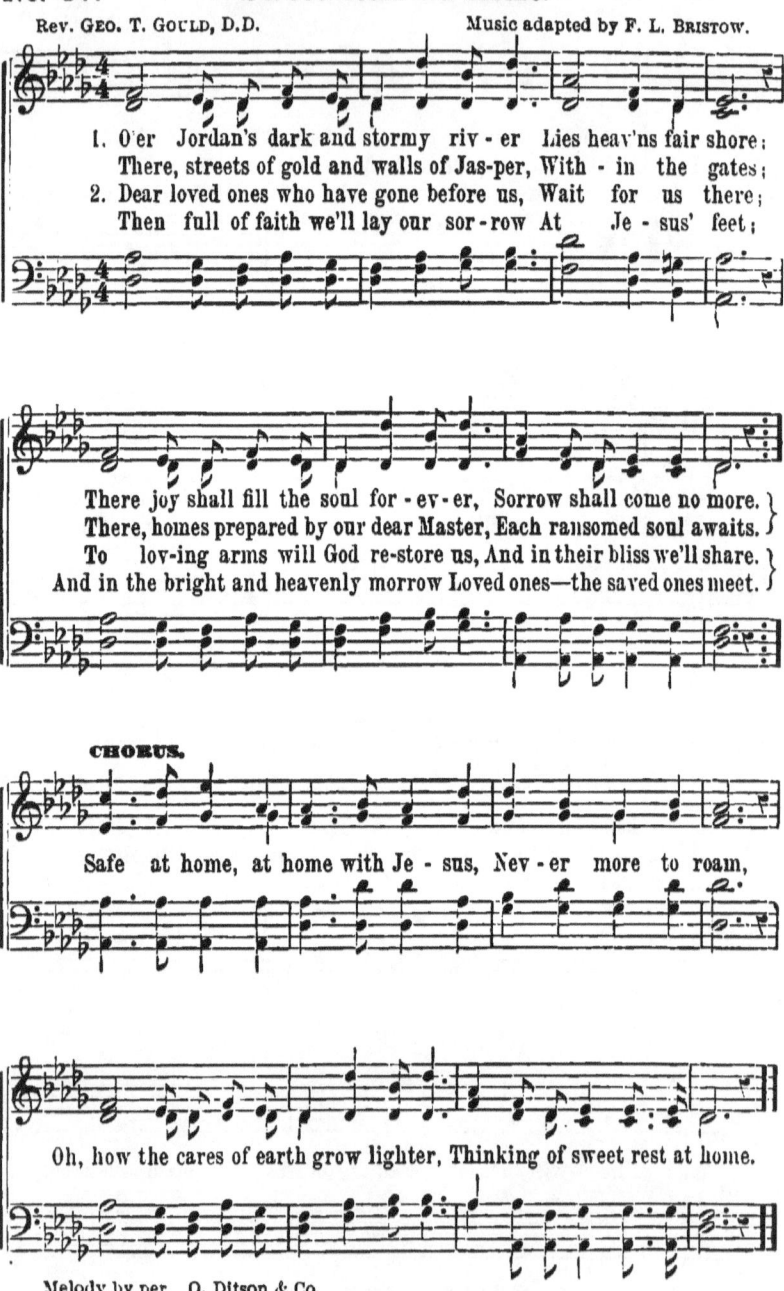

No. 58. I Could Not Do Without Thee.

FRANCES RIDLEY HAVERGAL. J. R. MURRAY, by per.

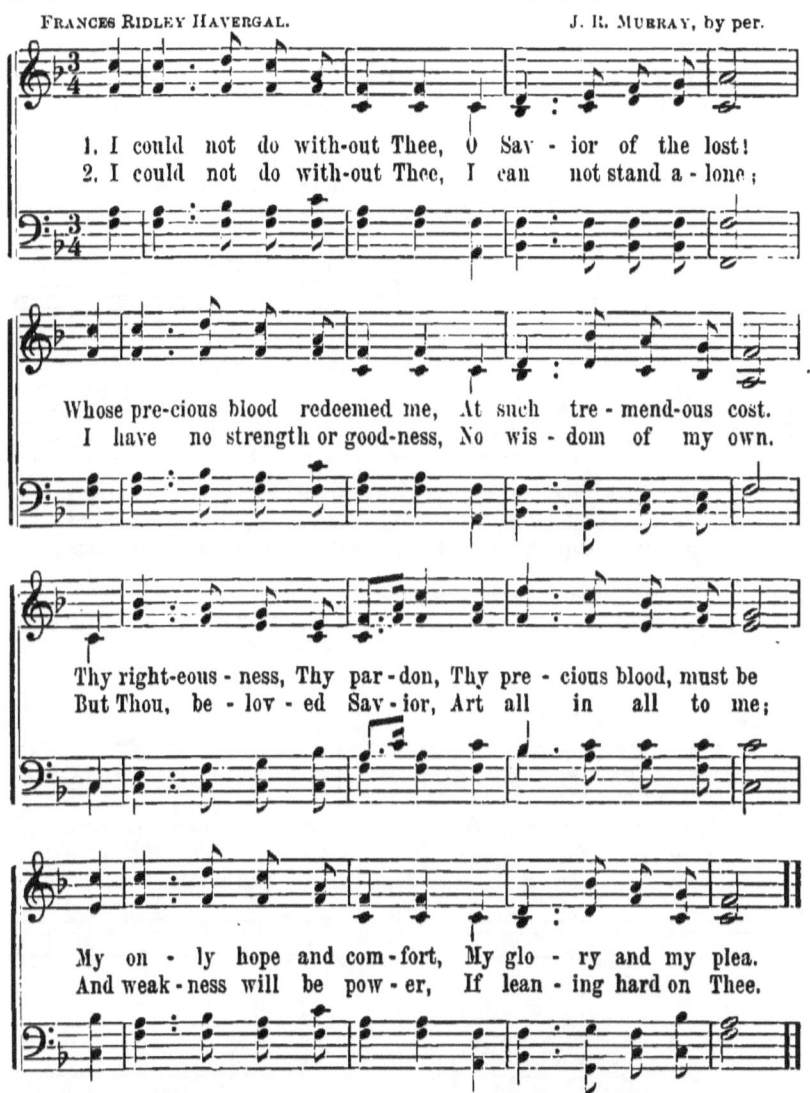

1. I could not do with-out Thee, O Sav-ior of the lost!
2. I could not do with-out Thee, I can not stand a-lone;

Whose pre-cious blood redeemed me, At such tre-mend-ous cost.
I have no strength or good-ness, No wis-dom of my own.

Thy right-eous-ness, Thy par-don, Thy pre-cious blood, must be
But Thou, be-lov-ed Sav-ior, Art all in all to me;

My on-ly hope and com-fort, My glo-ry and my plea.
And weak-ness will be pow-er, If lean-ing hard on Thee.

3 I could not do without Thee,
  For oh, the way is long,
And I am often weary,
  And sigh replaces song.
How could I do without Thee?
  I do not know the way;
Thou knowest and Thou leadest,
  And wilt not let me stray.

4 I could not do without Thee,
  For years are fleeting fast.
And soon, in solemn loneliness,
  The river must be passed.
But Thou wilt never leave me.
  And though the waves roll high,
I know Thou wilt be near me,
  And whisper, "It is I,"

No. 60. **Only Trust Him.**

"Take my yoke upon you, and learn of me; and ye shall find rest unto your souls."—MATT. 11: 29.

Rev. J. H. S.   Rev. J. H. Stockton, by per.

3 Yes, Jesus is the Truth, the Way,
That leads you into rest;
Believe in Him without delay,
And you are fully blest.

4 Come then, and join this holy band,
And on to glory go,
To dwell in that celestial land,
Where joys immortal flow.

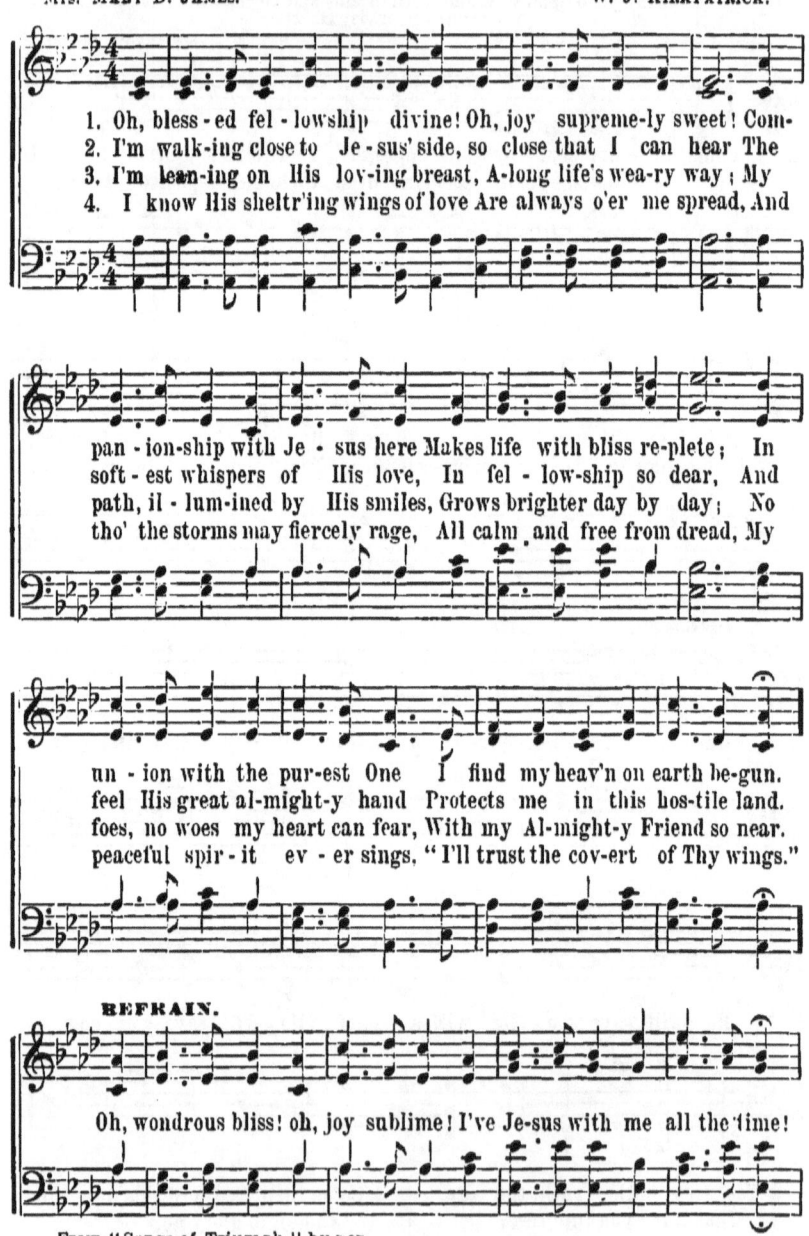

Companionship with Jesus. Concluded.

Oh, wondrous bliss! oh, joy sublime, I've Jesus with me all the time.

No. 62. Rejoicing Evermore.

R. E. HUDSON.

1. Tho' troubles assail, and dangers affright, Tho' friends should all
2. The birds, without barn or storehouse are fed; From them let us
3. When Satan appears to stop up our path, And fills us with
4. He tells us we're weak,—our hope is in vain; The good that we

CHORUS. Yes, I will rejoice, rejoice in the Lord; Yes, I will re-

fail, and foes all unite, Yet one thing secures us, whatever be-
learn to trust for our bread: His saints what is fitting shall ne'er be de-
fears we triumph by faith; He can not take from us, (tho' oft he has
seek we ne'er shall obtain: But when such suggestions our graces have

joice, rejoice in the Lord; Yes, I will rejoice, rejoice in the

tide, The promise assures us,—The Lord will provide.
nied, So long as 'tis written,—The Lord will provide.
tried) The heart-cheering promise,—The Lord will provide.
tried, This answers all questions,—The Lord will provide.

Lord, Will joy in the God of my salvation.

Copyright, 1882, by R. E. HUDSON.

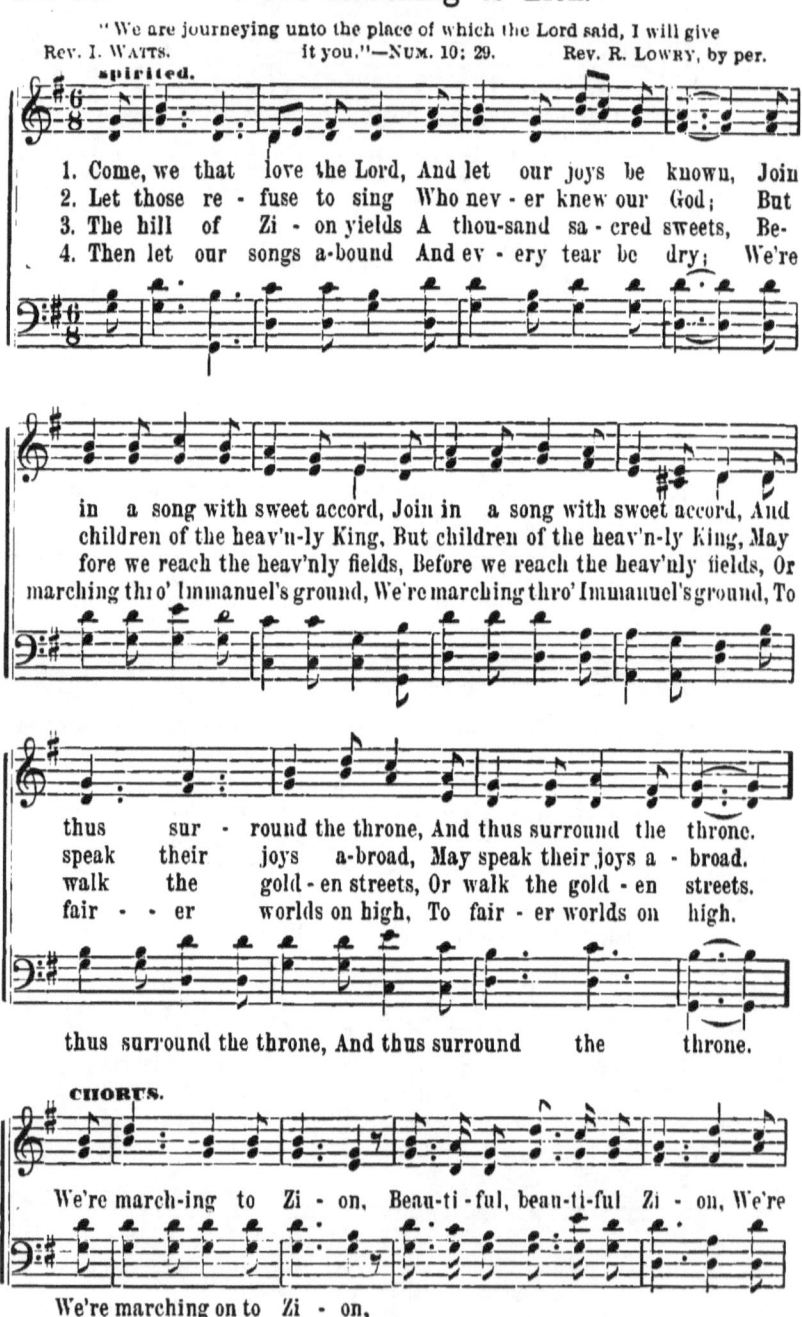

We're Marching to Zion. Concluded.

marching up-ward to Zi - on, The beauti-ful cit - y of God.
Zi - on, Zi - on,

No. 64.   **Webb.**   **7s & 6s, Double.**

G. J. WEBB.

1. The morn-ing light is break - ing, The darkness dis - ap-pears;
The sons of earth are wak - ing To pen - i - ten - tial tears;
D. S. Of na - tions in com-mo - tion, Prepared for Zi - on's war.
Each breeze that sweeps the o - cean Brings tidings from a - far,

2 See heathen nations bending
   Before the God we love,
And thousand hearts ascending
   In gratitude above;
While sinners, now confessing,
   The Gospel call obey,
And seek the Savior's blessing—
   A nation in a day.

3 Blest river of salvation!
   Pursue thine onward way;
Flow thou to every nation,
   Nor in thy richness stay;
Stay not till all the lowly
   Triumphant reach their home,
Stay not till all the holy
   Proclaim "The Lord is come."

Bringing in the Sheaves. Concluded.

We shall come, rejoicing, Bringing in the sheaves, Bringing in the sheaves, Bringing in the sheaves, We shall come, rejoicing, Bringing in the sheaves.

No. 68.   Warwick.   C. M

Rev. JOHN NEWTON, 1779.   SAMUEL STANLEY.

1. A - mazing grace, how sweet the sound, That saved a wretch like me!
2. 'Twas grace that taught my heart to fear, And grace my fears relieved;

I once was lost, but now am found; Was blind, but now I see.
How precious did that grace ap-pear, The hour I first be-lieved.

3 Thro' many dangers, toils, and snares,
I have already come:
'Tis grace that brought me safe thus far,
And grace will lead me home.

4 Yes, when this heart and flesh shall
And mortal life shall cease,   [fail,
I shall possess, within the vail
A life of joy and peace.

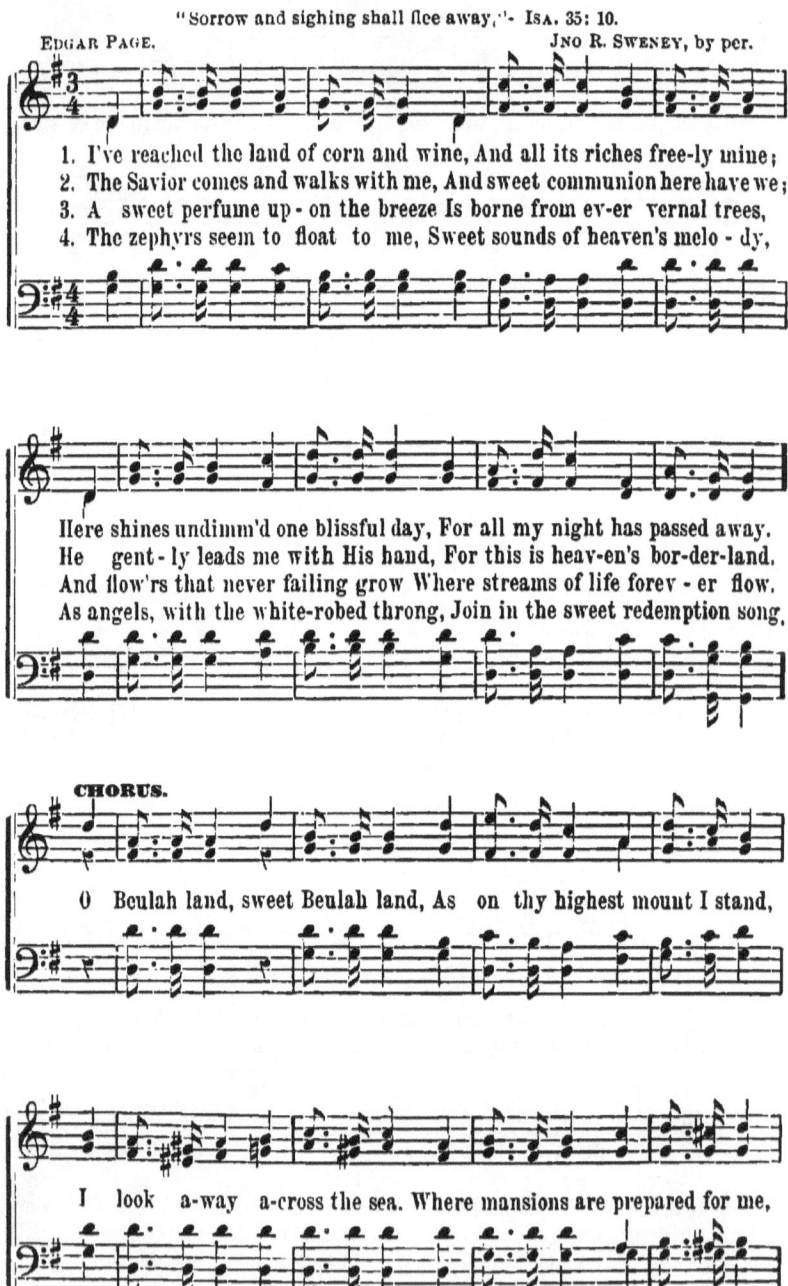

Beulah Land. Concluded.

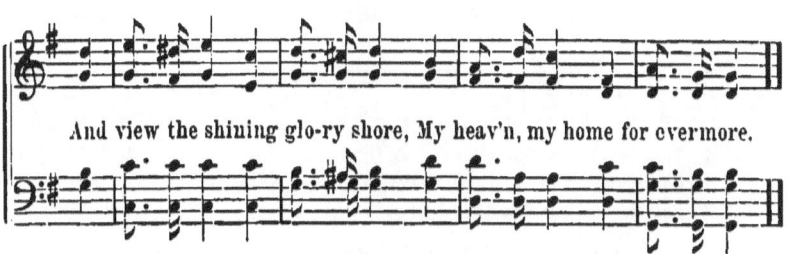

And view the shining glo-ry shore, My heav'n, my home for evermore.

No. 70. Just for To-day.

J. R. M. New arr. J. R. MURRAY.

1. Lord, for to-mor-row and its needs I do not pray; Keep me, my
2. Keep me from wrong in thought or deed, O Lord, I pray; Be near me
3. And when Thy summons comes to me, Calling a - way, Lend me Thy

God, from sin Just for to - day. Let me be glad to do Thy will,
in my need, Just for to - day. When storm-clouds gather darkly round,
helping hand Just for to - day. So for to-morrow and its needs

Prompt to o - bey, Give me Thy helping grace Just for to - day,
And hide my way. Be Thou, my light, O Lord, Just for to - day.
I do not pray; But keep me, guide me, Lord, Just for to - day.

Copyright, 1886, by THE JOHN CHURCH CO.

No. 71. Seeking to Save.

"For the Son of Man is come to seek and save that which was lost."—LUKE 19: 10.

P. P. B.
P. P. BLISS, by per.

1. Ten-der-ly the Shepherd, O'er the mountains cold, Goes to bring his
2. Pa-tient-ly the own-er Seeks with earnest care, In the dust and
3. Lov-ing-ly the Fa-ther Sends the news around: "He, once dead, now

CHORUS.

lost one Back to the fold.
darkness Her treasure rare.   Seeking to save, Seeking to save,
liv-eth—Once lost is found.

Lost one, 'tis Je-sus Seeking to save, Seek-ing to save,

Seek-ing to save, Lost one, 'tis Je-sus Seek-ing to save.

No. 73.   I've Washed My Robes.

E. O. E.   E. O. EXCELL.

1. My robes were once all stain'd with sin, I knew not how to make them clean;
1. That promise, "whoso-ev-er will," In-clud-ed me—includes me still;

Un-til a voice said, sweet and low, "Go wash, I'll make them white as snow."
I came, and ev-er since, I know, His blood, it cleanseth white as snow.

CHORUS.

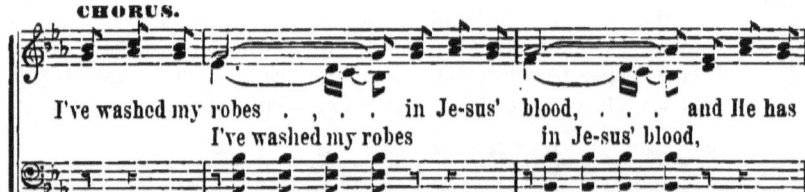

I've washed my robes . . . . in Jesus' blood, . . . and He has
I've washed my robes   in Jesus' blood,

made . . them white as snow: . . I've washed my robes, . . in Jesus'
And He has made   them white as snow: I've washed my robes

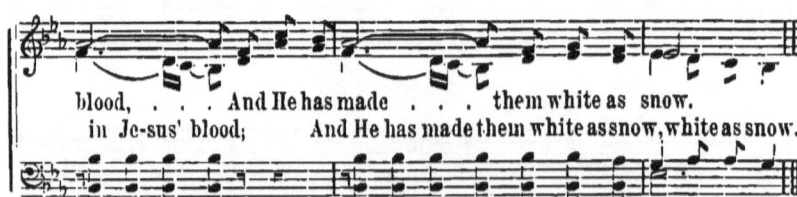

blood, . . . And He has made . . . them white as snow.
in Jesus' blood;   And He has made them white as snow, white as snow.

3 I do not doubt, nor do I say,
 "I hope the stains are washed away,"
 For in His Word I read it so:
 His blood it cleanseth white as snow.

4 Oh, who will come and wash to-day,
 'Till all their stains are washed away;
 Until by faith they see and know
 Their robes are washed as white as snow?

Copyright, 1882, by E. O. EXCELL.

No. 74. Almost.

Mrs. O. F. Walton.
Jno. R. Sweney, by per.

1. So near the door, and the door stood wide? Close to the port, but not in-side! Near to the fold, yet not with-in, Al-most re-solved to give up sin! Al-most per-suad-ed to count the cost, Al-most a Christian, and yet lost?

2. Lord, help me trust in Thy word to-day, That Thou art the Light, the Truth, the Way. Now as I come, with my load of sin, The door be-ing o-pen, oh, help me step in. How sad the thought that for me, at last, The door should be shut, and mer-cy past!

3. Sav-ior, I come, I cry un-to Thee, Oh, let not these words be true of me, I want to come to the point to-day. Oh, suf-fer me not to turn a-way; Give me no rest, till my soul shall be With-in the Ref-uge,—safe with Thee.

No. 76.   **Tell it to Jesus Alone.**

"Tell it to Jesus."—MATT. 14: 12.

J. E. RANKIN, D. D.   Rev. E. S. LORENZ, by per.

1. Are you wea-ry, are you heav-y-heart-ed? Tell it to Je-sus,
2. Do the tears flow down your cheeks unbid-den? Tell it to Je-sus,
3. Do you fear the gath'ring clouds of sor-row? Tell it to Je-sus,
4. Are you troubled at the tho't of dy-ing, Tell it to Je-sus,

Tell it to Je-sus; Are you griev-ing o-ver joys de-part-ed?
Tell it to Je-sus; Have you sins that to man's eye are hid-den?
Tell it to Je-sus; Are you anx-ious what shall be to-mor-row?
Tell it to Je-sus; For Christ's com-ing Kingdom are you sigh-ing?

CHORUS.

Tell it to Je-sus a-lone. Tell it to Je-sus, Tell it to Je-sus,
He is a friend that's well known; You have no oth-er
such a friend or broth-er? Tell it to Je-sus a-lone.

Copyright, 1880, by E. S. LORENZ.

No. 77. **Is My Name Written There?**

"Rejoice because your names are written in heaven."—LUKE. 10: 20.

Mrs. MARY A. KIDDER. FRANK M. DAVIS, by per.

1. Lord, I care not for riches, Neither silver nor gold; I would make sure of heav-en, I would enter the fold. In the book of Thy kingdom, With its pag-es so fair, Tell me, Jesus, my Savior, Is my name written there?
2. Lord, my sins they are many, Like the sands of the sea, But Thy blood, O my Sav-ior! Is suf-fi-cient for me; For Thy promise is written, In bright letters that glow, "Tho' your sins be as scarlet, I will make them like snow."
3. Oh! the beautiful city, With its mansions of light, With its glo-ri-fied be-ings, In pure garments of white; Where no evil thing cometh, To despoil what is fair; Where the angels are watching, Yes, my name's written there.

CHORUS.

Is my name writ-ten there, On the page white and fair?

Chorus for 2d and 3d verses.
Yes, my name's, etc.

Is My Name Written There? Concluded.

In the book of Thy king-dom, Is my name writ-ten there?
2d and 3d verses.
Yes, my name's writ-ten there.

No. 78. Take Me as I Am.

Melody by the late Rev. J. H. Stockton. Har. by W. J. K, by per.

1. Je-sus, my Lord, to Thee I cry, Unless Thou help me I must die;
2. Helpless I am, and full of guilt, But yet for me Thy blood was spilt,

Oh, bring Thy free sal-va-tion nigh, And take me as I am!
And Thou can'st make me what Thou wilt, But take me as I am!

D.S. bring Thy free sal-va-tion nigh, And take me as I am!

REFRAIN.

Take me as I am, Take me as I am; Oh,
Take me as I am, Take me as I am;

3 No preparation can I make,
My best resolves I only break,
Yet save me for Thine own name's sake,
And take me as I am!

4 I thirst, I long to know Thy love,
Thy full salvation I would prove;
But since to Thee I can not move,
Oh, take me as I am!

5 If Thou hast work for me to do,
Inspire my will, my heart renew,
And work both in and by me too.
But take me as I am!

6 And when at last the work is done,
The battle o'er, the vict'ry won,
Still, still my cry shall be alone,
Lord, take me as I am!

No. 82. Let Him In.

Rev. J. B. Atchinson. E. O. Excell, by per.

1. There's a stranger at the door,
2. O-pen now to him your heart,
3. Hear you now His loving voice?
4. Now admit the heav'nly Guest,

He has been there oft be-fore,
If you wait He will de-part,
Now, oh, now make Him your choice,
He will make for you a feast.

Let Him in, ere He is gone, Let Him in, the Ho-ly One, Je-sus
Let Him in, He is your Friend, He your soul will sure de-fend, He will
He is standing at the door, Joy to you He will re-store, And His
He will speak your sins forgiven, And when earth ties all are riven, He will

Christ, the Father's Son,
keep you to the end.
name you will a-dore,
take you home to heaven.

No. 83 — The Solid Rock.

"The Lord is my defence, and rock of my refuge."—Ps. 94: 22.

Rev. EDWARD MOTE, 1825. WM. B. BRADBURY, by per.

1. My hope is built on nothing less Than Jesus' blood and righteousness;
2. When darkness veils His lovely face, I rest on his unchanging grace;
3. His oath, His cov-e-nant, His blood, Support me in the whelming flood;
4. When He shall come with trumpet sound, Oh, may I then in Him be found;

I dare not trust the sweetest frame, But wholly lean on Je-sus' name.
In every high and stormy gale, My anchor holds within the vail.
When all around my soul gives way, He then is all my hope and stay.
Drest in His righteousness a-lone, Faultless to stand before the throne!

CHORUS.

On Christ, the Sol-id Rock, I stand; All oth-er ground is sink-ing sand, All oth-er ground is sink-ing sand.

No. 84. Over the Threshold.

FRANK GOULD.   JNO. R. SWENEY.

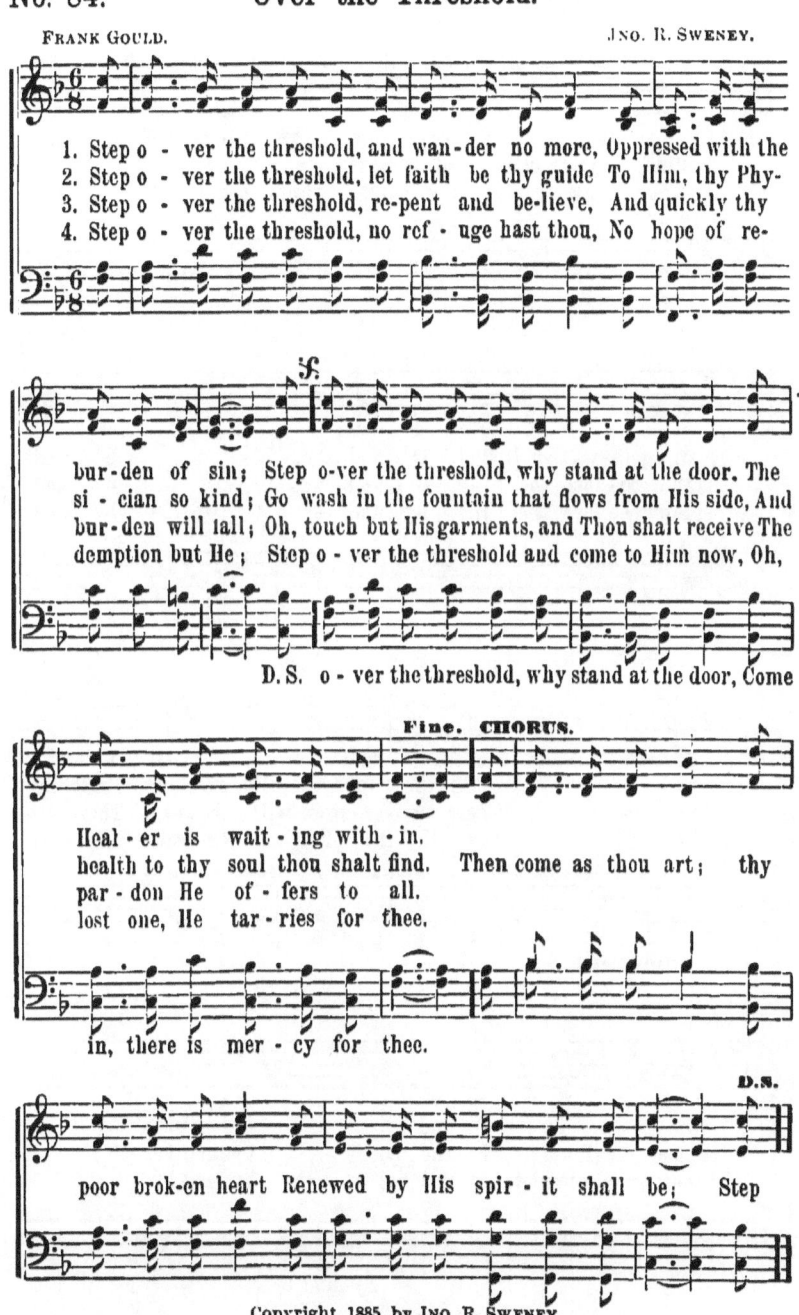

1. Step o-ver the threshold, and wan-der no more, Oppressed with the bur-den of sin; Step o-ver the threshold, why stand at the door. The Heal-er is wait-ing with-in.
2. Step o-ver the threshold, let faith be thy guide To Him, thy Phy-si-cian so kind; Go wash in the fountain that flows from His side, And health to thy soul thou shalt find.
3. Step o-ver the threshold, re-pent and be-lieve, And quickly thy bur-den will fall; Oh, touch but His garments, and Thou shalt receive The par-don He of-fers to all.
4. Step o-ver the threshold, no ref-uge hast thou, No hope of re-demption but He; Step o-ver the threshold and come to Him now, Oh, lost one, He tar-ries for thee.

CHORUS.

Then come as thou art; thy poor brok-en heart Renewed by His spir-it shall be; Step o-ver the threshold, why stand at the door, Come in, there is mer-cy for thee.

Copyright, 1885, by JNO. R. SWENEY.

No. 85. We Shall Stand Before the King.

E. O. E.
E. O. Excell.

1. We shall stand be-fore the King, With the an-gels we shall sing, By and by, . . . by and by. Walk the bright, the gold-en shore, Prais-ing Him for ev-ermore, By and by, . . . by and by.
2. Ring, ye bells of heav-en, ring, We shall stand be-fore the King, By and by, . . . by and by. There our sor-rows will be o'er, There His name we will a-dore, By and by, . . . by and by.
3. Wake, my soul, thy tri-bute bring, Thou shalt stand be-fore the King, By and by, . . . by and by. Lay thy tro-phies at His feet, In His likeness stand complete, By and by, . . . by and by.

Copyright, 1885, by E. O. Excell.

We Shall Stand Before the King. Concluded.

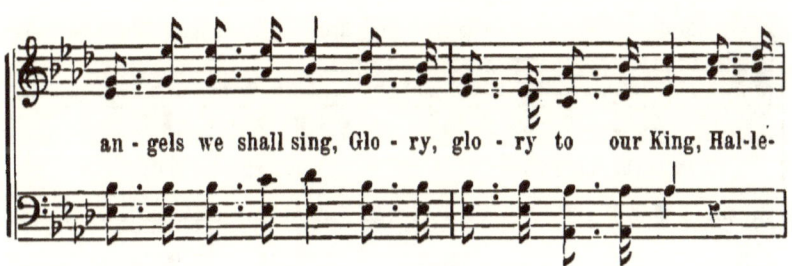

No. 86. Calvary.

"The place which is called Calvary, there they crucified Him."—LUKE 23:33.

Rev. W. M'K. Darwood.   Jno. R. Sweney, by per.

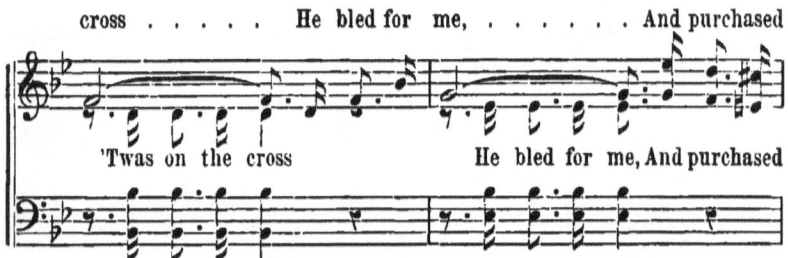

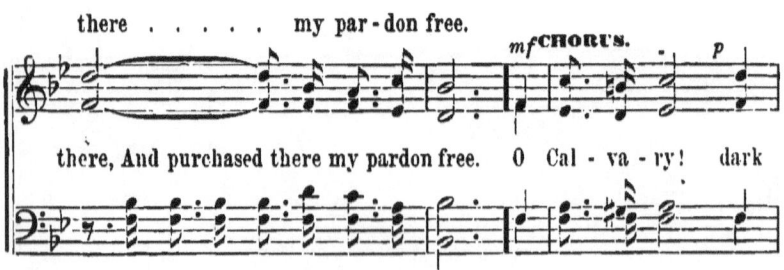

Copyright, 1886, by Jno. R. Sweney.

Calvary. Concluded.

2 'Mid rending rocks and dark'ning skies,
My Savior bows His head and dies;
The opening vale reveals the way
To heaven's joys and endless day.

3 O Jesus, Lord, how can it be,
That Thou shouldst give Thy life for me,
To bear the cross and agony,—
In that dread hour on Calvary!—

No. 87.   Cross and Crown.

"And he bearing his cross, went forth."—JOHN 19: 17.

THOS. SHEPHERD.   GEO. N. ALLEN, 1849, by per.

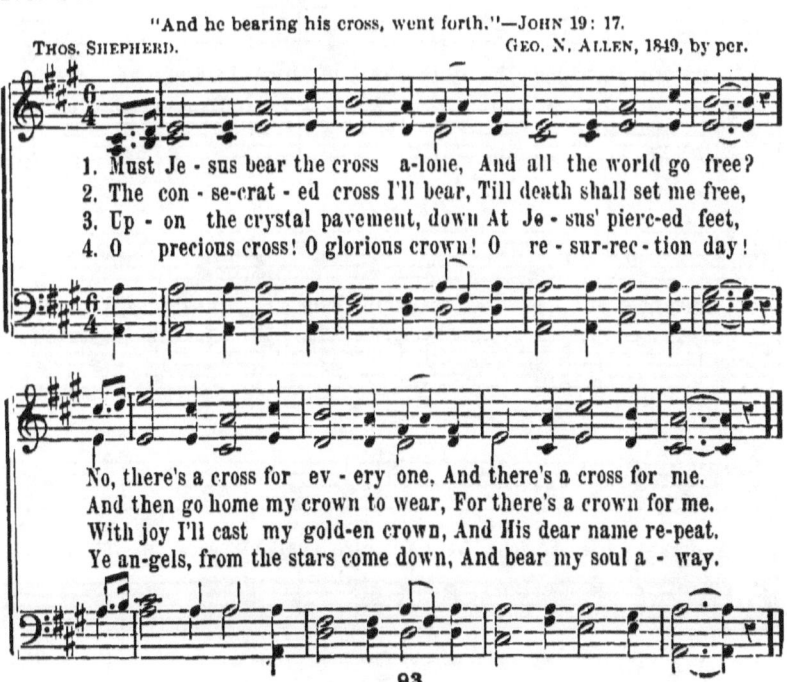

1. Must Jesus bear the cross alone, And all the world go free?
2. The consecrated cross I'll bear, Till death shall set me free,
3. Upon the crystal pavement, down At Jesus' pierced feet,
4. O precious cross! O glorious crown! O resurrection day!

No, there's a cross for every one, And there's a cross for me.
And then go home my crown to wear, For there's a crown for me.
With joy I'll cast my golden crown, And His dear name repeat.
Ye angels, from the stars come down, And bear my soul away.

No. 89. The Half was Never Told.

"Behold, the half was not told."—KINGS 10: 7.

P. P. B.
P. P. BLISS, by per.

1. Re-peat the sto-ry o'er and o'er, Of grace so full and free; I love to hear it more and more, Since grace has rescued me.
2. Of peace I on-ly knew the name, Nor found my soul its rest Un-til the sweet-voiced angels came To soothe my wea-ry breast.
3. My high-est place is ly-ing low At my Re-deem-er's feet; No re-al joy in life I know, But in His serv-ice sweet.
4. And oh, what rapture will it be With all the host a-bove, To sing through all e-ter-ni-ty The won-ders of His love.

CHORUS.

The half was nev-er told, The half was nev-er told, The half was nev-er told, never told, never told, The half was never told.

1. Of grace divine, so wonderful, The half was nev-er, nev-er told.
2. Of peace, etc.
3. Of joy, etc.
4. Of love, etc.

No. 91. Redeeming Love.

J. R. MURRAY.

1. My soul re-joic-ing fain would raise A strain like that a-bove,
2. When dark-ly bend the clouds of life, And loud its tempests roll,
3. Re-deem-ing love! Thou blest re-frain! Let mor-tal mu-sic cease

And sing in grate-ful har-mon-ies Of God's re-deem-ing love.
How like a ben-e-dic-tion calm Thy power up-on my soul.
While an-gels o'er the list'ning earth Pro-long thy notes of peace.

CHORUS.

Re-deem-ing love! Re-deem-ing love! A sto-ry nev-er old;

Still sweet-er as the years go by, Still bright as burnished gold.

Copyright, 1886, by THE JOHN CHURCH CO.

No. 93. Jesus is Calling.

FANNY J. CROSBY.   GEO. C. STEBBINS, by per.

3 Jesus is waiting, oh, come to Him now—
  Waiting to-day, waiting to-day;
  Come with thy sins, at His feet lowly bow
  Come, and no longer delay.

4 Jesus is pleading, oh, list to His voice—
  Hear Him to-day, Hear Him to-day;
  They who believe on His name shall rejoice;
  Quickly arise and away.

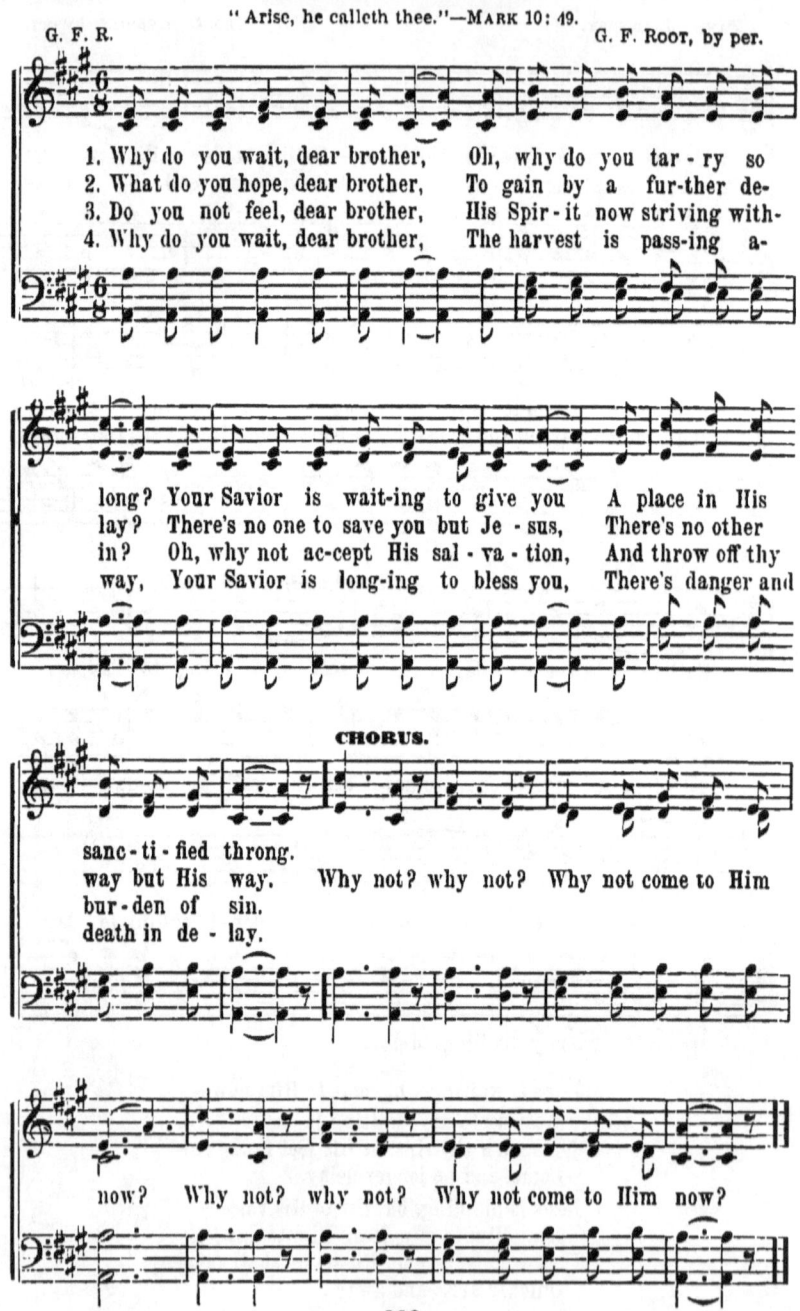

No. 95. **Who'll be the Next.**

ANNIE S. HAWKS.   Rev. ROBERT LOWRY, by per.

1. Who'll be the next to fol-low Jesus? Who'll be the next the cross to bear?
2. Who'll be the next to fol-low Jesus—Fol-low his wea-ry, bleeding feet?

Some one is ready, some one is waiting; Who'll be the next a crown to wear?
Who'll be the next to lay every burden Down at the Father's mer-cy-seat?

REFRAIN.

Who'll be the next? Who'll be the next? Who'll be the next to follow Je-sus?

Who'll be the next to fol-low Je-sus now? Fol-low Je-sus now?

3 Who'll be the next to follow Jesus?
   Who'll be the next to praise His name?
   Who'll swell the chorus of free redemption—
   Sing, hallelujah! praise the Lamb?

4 Who'll be the next to follow Jesus,
   Down through the Jordan's rolling tide?
   Who'll be the next to join with the ransomed,
   Singing upon the other side?

101

No. 96. What a Friend We Have in Jesus.

"There is a Friend that sticketh closer than a brother."—PROV. 18: 24.

ANON.   CHARLES C. CONVERSE, by per.

1. What a Friend we have in Je-sus, All our sins and griefs to bear;
2. Have we tri-als and temp-ta-tions? Is there trouble an-y-where?
3. Are we weak and heav-y-la-den, Cumbered with a load of care?

What a priv-i-lege to car-ry Ev-'rything to God in prayer.
We should nev-er be dis-cour-aged, Take it to the Lord in prayer.
Pre-cious Sav-ior, still our ref-uge—Take it to the Lord in prayer.

Oh, what peace we oft-en for-feit, Oh, what needless pain we bear—
Can we find a Friend so faith-ful, Who will all our sorrows share?
Do thy friends despise, forsake thee? Take it to the Lord in prayer;

All be-cause we do not car-ry Ev-'rything to God in prayer.
Je-sus knows our ev-'ry weakness, Take it to the Lord in prayer.
In His arms He'll take and shield thee, Take it to the Lord in prayer.

No. 97.   **The Great Physician.**

"Is there no balm in Gilead; is there no physician there?"—JER. 8: 22.

Rev. WM. HUNTER.   Arr. by Rev. J. H. STOCKTON.

1. The great Physi-cian now is near, The sym-pa-thiz-ing Je - sus,
2. Your many sins are all forgiven, Oh, hear the voice of Je - sus;
3. All glo-ry to the dy-ing Lamb! I now be-lieve in Je - sus;

He speaks, the drooping heart to cheer, Oh, hear the voice of Je - sus.
Go on your way in peace to heaven, And wear a crown with Je - sus.
I love the bless-ed Savior's name, I love the name of Je - sus.

CHORUS.

"Sweetest note in se-raph song, Sweetest name on mor-tal tongue,

Rit.

Sweet-est car - ol ev - er sung, Je - sus, bless-ed Je - sus."

4 The children too, both great and small,
   Who love the name of Jesus,
May now accept the gracious call
   To work and live for Jesus.

5 Come, brethren, help me sing His praise,
   Oh, praise the name of Jesus;
Come, sisters, all your voices raise,
   Oh, bless the name of Jesus.

6 His name dispels my guilt and fear,
   No other name but Jesus;
Oh, how my soul delights to hear
   The precious name of Jesus.

7 And when to that bright world above,
   We rise to see our Jesus,
We'll sing around the throne of love
   His name, the name of Jesus.

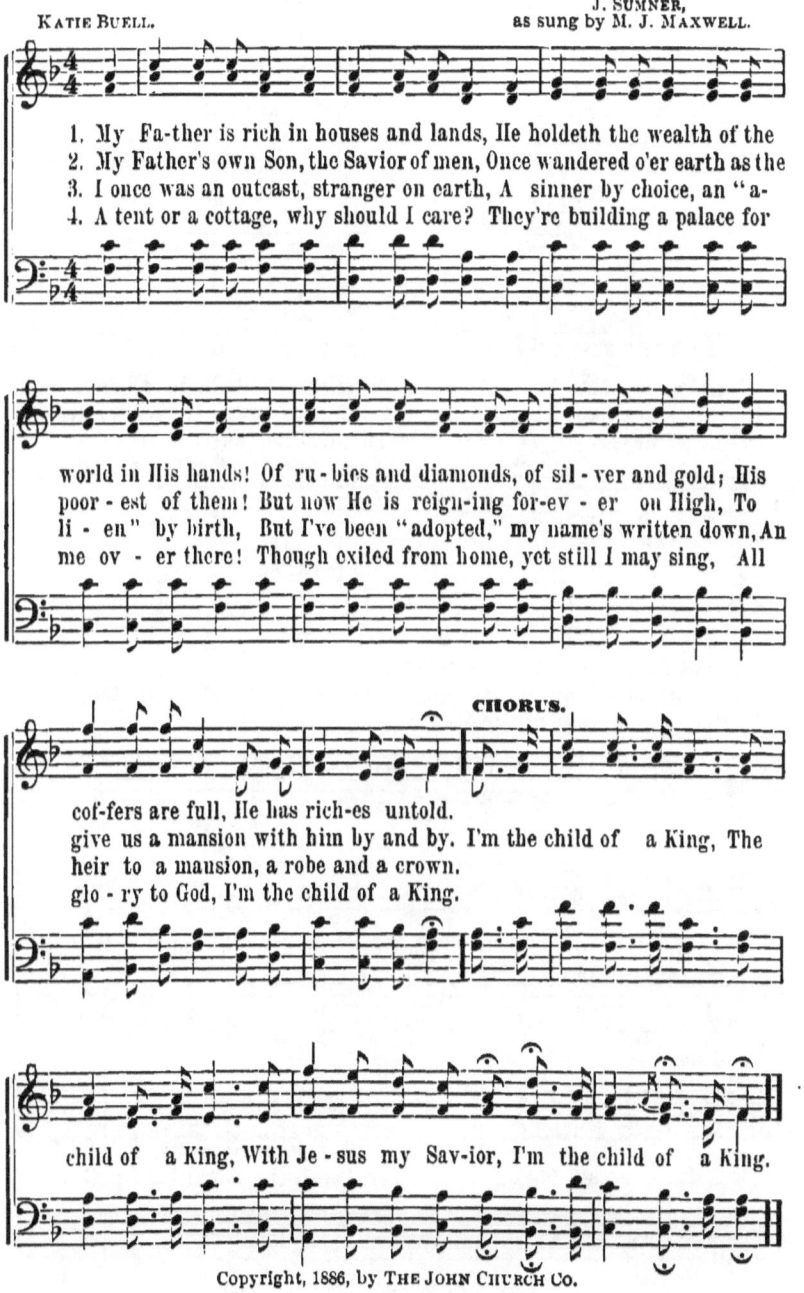

Meet Me There. Concluded.

Tree of Life is blooming, Meet me there. When the Tree of Life is blooming, Meet me there.

No. 103. Dare to be a Daniel.

"But Daniel purposed in his heart that he would not defile himself with the portion of the king's meat, nor with the wine which he drank.—DAN. 1: 8.

P. P. B.   P. P. BLISS, by per.

1. Stand-ing by a pur-pose true, Heed-ing God's command,
2. Ma-ny might-y men are lost, Dar-ing not to stand,
3. Ma-ny gi-ants, great and tall, Stalk-ing thro' the land,
4. Hold the gos-pel ban-ner high! On to vic-t'ry grand!

Hon-or them, the faith-ful few! All hail to Dan-iel's Band!
Who for God had been a host, By join-ing Dan-iel's Band.
Head-long to the earth would fall, If met by Dan-iel's Band.
Sa-tan and his host de-fy, And shout for Dan-iel's Band.

CHORUS.

Dare to be a Dan-iel, Dare to stand a-lone!
Dare to have a pur-pose firm! Dare to make it known.

No. 104. Jesus will Help You.

"Grace to help in time of need."—HEB. 4: 16.

WM. STEVENSON. R. LOWRY, by per.

1. The Sav-ior is call-ing you, sin-ner—Urg-ing you now to draw nigh;
2. Thro' Him there is life in be-liev-ing; Sin-ner, oh, why will you die?
3. There's danger in longer de-lay-ing, Swift-ly the moments pass by;

He asks you by faith to re-ceive Him, Je-sus will help if you try.
Ac-cept Him by faith as your Sav-ior, Je-sus will help if you try.
If now you will come there is mer-cy, Je-sus will help if you try.

REFRAIN.

Jesus will help you, Jesus will help you, Help you with grace from on high; The

weakest and poorest the Savior is calling, Je-sus will help if you try.

No. 106. Where is my Boy To-night?

"A foolish boy is the heaviness of his mother."— PROV. 10: 1.

R. L.   **With tenderness.**   Rev. ROBERT LOWRY, by per.

1. Where is my wand'ring boy to-night—The boy of my tend'rest care, The boy that was once my joy and light, The child of my love and prayer?
2. Once he was pure as morning dew, As he knelt at his mother's knee; No face was so bright, no heart more true, And none was so sweet as he.
3. Oh, could I see you now, my boy, As fair as in old-en time, When prattle and smile made home a joy, And life was a mer-ry chime.
4. Go for my wand'ring boy to-night; Go search for him where you will; But bring him to me with all his blight, And tell him I love him still.

CHORUS. *Not too fast.*

Oh, where is my boy to-night? Oh, where is my boy to-night? My heart o'erflows, for I love him, he knows; Oh, where is my boy to-night?

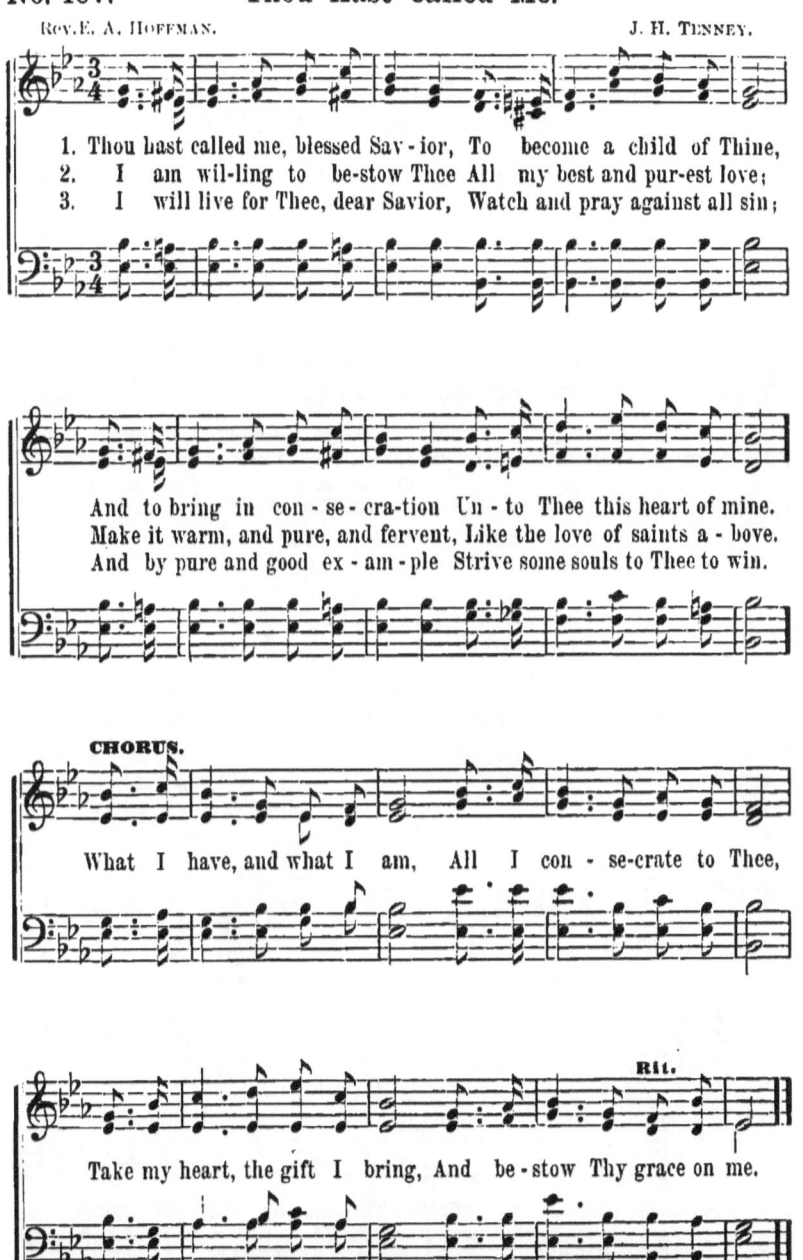

No. 108. Scatter Seeds of Kindness.

"Be kindly affectioned one to another."—Rom. 12: 10.

Mrs. Albert Smith.   S. J. Vail, by per.

1. Let us gath-er up the sunbeams Ly-ing all a-round our path; Let us keep the wheat and ros-es, Cast-ing out the thorns and chaff. Let us find our sweet-est com-fort In the blessings of to-day, With a pa-tient hand re-moving All the bri-ars from the way.

2. Strange we nev-er prize the mu-sic Till the sweet-voiced bird is flown! Strange that we should slight the vio-lets Till the love-ly flow'rs are gone! Strange that summer skies and sunshine Nev-er seem one-half so fair, As when winter's snow-y pinions Shake the white down in the air.

CHORUS.

Then scat-ter seeds of kindness, Then scat-ter seeds of kindness,

Scatter Seeds of Kindness. Concluded.

3 If we knew the baby fingers,
  Pressed against the window pane,
Would be cold and stiff to-morrow—
  Never trouble us again—
Would the bright eyes of our darling
  Catch the frown upon our brow?—
Would the prints of rosy fingers
  Vex us then as they do now?

4 Ah! those little ice-cold fingers,
  How they point our memories back
To the hasty words and actions
  Strewn along our backward track!
How those little hands remind us,
  As in snowy grace they lie,
Not to scatter thorns—but roses—
  For our reaping by and by.

No. 109.   Just as I Am.   L. M.

"Him that cometh unto Me, I will in no wise cast out.—JOHN 6: 37.
Mrs. CHARLOTTE ELLIOT, 1834.   WM. B. BRADBURY, by per.

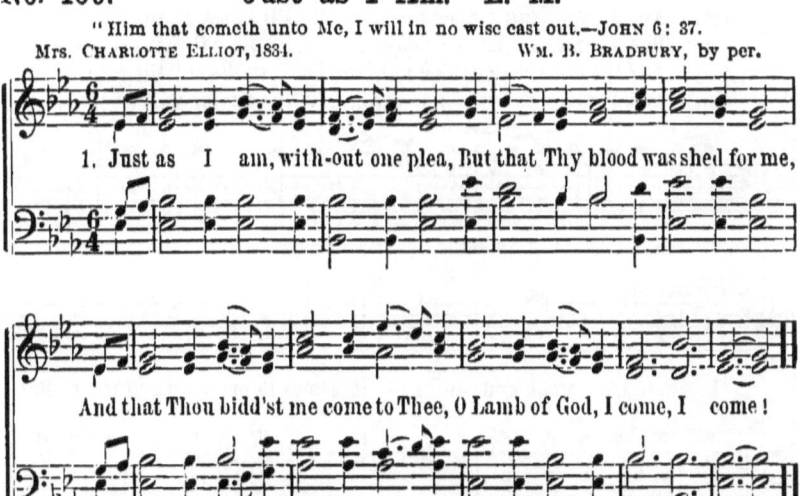

2 Just as I am, and waiting not
To rid my soul of one dark blot, (spot,
To Thee, whose blood can cleanse each
  O Lamb of God! I come, I come!

3 Just as I am, though tossed about,
With many a conflict, many a doubt,
Fightings and fears within, without,
  O Lamb of God! I come, I come!

4 Just as I am, poor, wretched, blind,
Sight, riches, healing of the mind,
Yes, all I need, in Thee to find,
  O Lamb of God! I come, I come!

5 Just as I am; Thou wilt receive,
Wilt welcome, pardon, cleanse, relieve,
Because Thy promise I believe,
  O Lamb of God! I come, I come!

No. 110. **The Mistakes of my Life.**

"Behold, I have set before thee an open door."—REV. 3: 8.

Mrs. URANIA LOCKE BAILEY. Rev. ROBERT LOWRY, by per.

Tenderly.

1. The mistakes of my life have been many, The sins of my heart have been
2. I am low-est of those who love Him, I am weak-est of those who
3. My mistakes His free grace will cover, My sins He will wash a-
4. The mistakes of my life have been many, And my spir-it is sick with

more, And I scarce can see for weeping, But I'll knock at the open door.
pray; But I come as He has bid-den, And He will not say me nay.
way, And the feet that shrink and falter Shall walk thro' the gates of day
sin, And I scarce can see for weeping, But the Savior will let me in.

CHORUS.

I know I am weak and sinful, It comes to me more and more; But

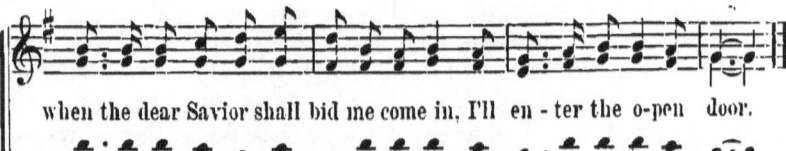

when the dear Savior shall bid me come in, I'll en-ter the o-pen door.

No. 112. Trusting Jesus, That is All.

EDGAR PAGE. JNO. R. SWENEY, by per.

3 Singing, if my way is clear;
Praying, if the path is drear;
If in danger, for Him call—
Trusting Jesus, that is all.

4 Trusting as the moments fly,
Trusting as the days go by,
Trusting Him, whate'er befall—
Trusting Jesus, that is all.

No. 113. Let the Master in.

"Behold, I stand at the door and knock; if any man hear my voice, and open the door, I will come in to him."—Rev. 3: 20.

Rev. S. D. Phelps, D.D.
R. Lowry., by per.

1. Once I heard a sound at my heart's dark door, And was roused from the slumber of sin; It was Jesus knocked, He had knocked before; Now I said, Blessed Master, come in.
2. Then He spread a feast of redeeming love, And He made me His own happy guest; In my joy I thought that the saints above Could be hardly more favored or blest.
3. In the holy war with the foes of truth, He's my Shield, He my table prepares, He restores my soul, He renews my youth, And gives triumph in answer to prayers.
4. He will feast me still with His presence dear, And the love He so freely hath given, While His promise tells, as I serve Him here, Of the banquet of glory in heaven.

CHORUS.

Then open, open, open, let the Master in, (let Him in;) For the heart will be bright with a heav'nly light, When you let the Master in.

No. 114. Who's on the Lord's Side?

"Who is on the Lord's side."—Ex. 32: 26.

Mrs. W. R. Griswold.   P. P. Bliss, by per.

1. We're marching to Canaan with ban-ner and song, We're soldiers en-list-ed to fight 'gainst the wrong; But, lest in the con-flict our strength should divide, We ask, who a-mong us is on the Lord's side?
2. The sword may be burnished, the armor be bright, For Sa-tan ap-pears as an an-gel of light; Yet dark-ly the bo-som may treach-e-ry hide, While lips are profess-ing, "I'm on the Lord's side."
3. Who is there among us yet un-der the rod, Who knows not the par-don-ing mer-cy of God? Oh, bring to Him hum-bly the heart in its pride; Oh, haste, while He's waiting and seek the Lord's side.

CHORUS.

Oh, who is there among us, the true and the tried, Who'll stand by His col-ors—who's on the Lord's side? Oh, who is there among us, the

Who's on the Lord's Side? Concluded.

true and the tried, Who'll stand by His col-ors—who's on the Lord's side?

4 Oh, heed not the sorrow, the pain and the wrong,
For soon shall our sighing, be changed into song;
So bearing the cross of our covenant Guide,
We'll shout as we triumph, "I'm on the Lord's side."

No. 115. Glory to His Name!

E. A. Hoffman.   Ps. 63: 4.   Rev. J. H. Stockton, by per.

1. Down at the cross where the Savior died, Down where for cleansing from
2. I am so wondrously saved from sin; Jesus so sweetly a-
3. Come to this fountain, so rich and sweet, Humble your soul at the

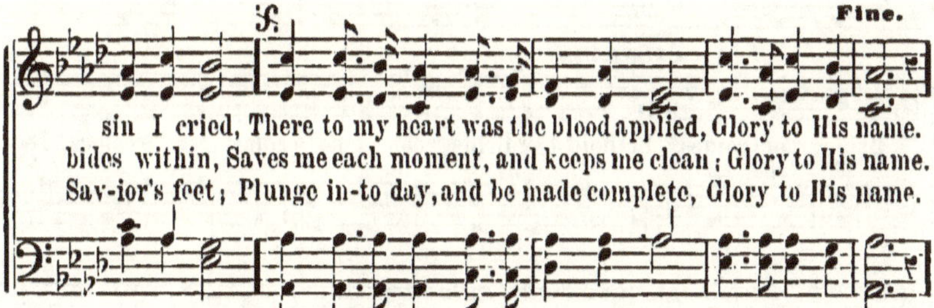

sin I cried, There to my heart was the blood applied, Glory to His name.
bides within, Saves me each moment, and keeps me clean; Glory to His name.
Sav-ior's feet; Plunge in-to day, and be made complete, Glory to His name.

D. S. Now to my heart is the blood ap-plied, Glory to His name.

CHORUS.
Glo-ry to His name! Glo-ry to His name!

No. 117. Jesus will Give You Rest.

FANNY CROSBY.   MATT 11: 28.   JNO. R. SWENEY, by per.

1. Will you come, will you come with your poor broken heart, Burden'd and sin-op-
2. Will you come, will you come? there is mercy for you, Balm for your ach-ing

pressed? Lay it down at the feet of the Sav-ior and Lord,
breast; On-ly come as you are, and be-lieve on His name,

CHORUS.

Je-sus will give you rest. O hap-py rest, sweet, hap-py rest!
Je-sus will give you rest.

Je-sus will give you rest, Oh! why won't you come in

hap-py rest,

sim-ple, trust-ing faith? Je-sus will give you rest.

3 Will you come, will you come? you
   have nothing to pay;
Jesus, who loves you best,
By His death on the Cross purchased
   life for your soul;
Jesus will give you rest.

4 Will you come, will you come? how
   He pleads with you now!
Fly to His loving breast;
And whatever your sin or your sorrow
   may be,
Jesus will give you rest.

No. 118. Trusting Jesus.

"Casting all your care upon Him, for He careth for you."—1 Peter 5: 7.

ALICE JACOBS. E. O. EXCELL.

1. Are you trusting in the Sav-ior, Trusting in His gracious care?
2. Wea-ry sin-ner, go to Je-sus, Tell Him of the fault with-in;
3. Do not fear, He will ac-cept you, For His prom-is-es are true;
4. Go, then, cast your cares upon Him, Bow-ing humbly at His feet;

Is your faith in Je-sus rest-ing? Does He ev-ery bur-den bear?
Nev-er doubt-ing, nev-er fear-ing, For His blood can cleanse all sin.
And He says He will not cast out A-ny sin-ner, e-ven you.
Then go forth to work for Je-sus, Conq'ring all the foes you meet.

REFRAIN.

He is a-ble, He is will-ing, He can bear your burdens all;
He is a-ble, He is willing,

He will save you, He will keep you, Come, then, heed His loving call.
He will save you, He will keep you,

Copyright, 1886, by E. O. Excell.

3 He can wash you white as snow,
  Will you be washed in the blood?
And the witness you may know,
  Will you be washed in the blood?
    You can know this hour
    Of His dying power.

4 Christ did drink that cup for all,
  Will you be washed in the blood?
Don't reject the Spirit's call,
  Will you be washed in the blood?
    Grace is all abounding,
    Joy through heaven resounding.

No. 120. The Call for Reapers.

J. R. THOMPSON. J. B. O. CLEMM, by per.

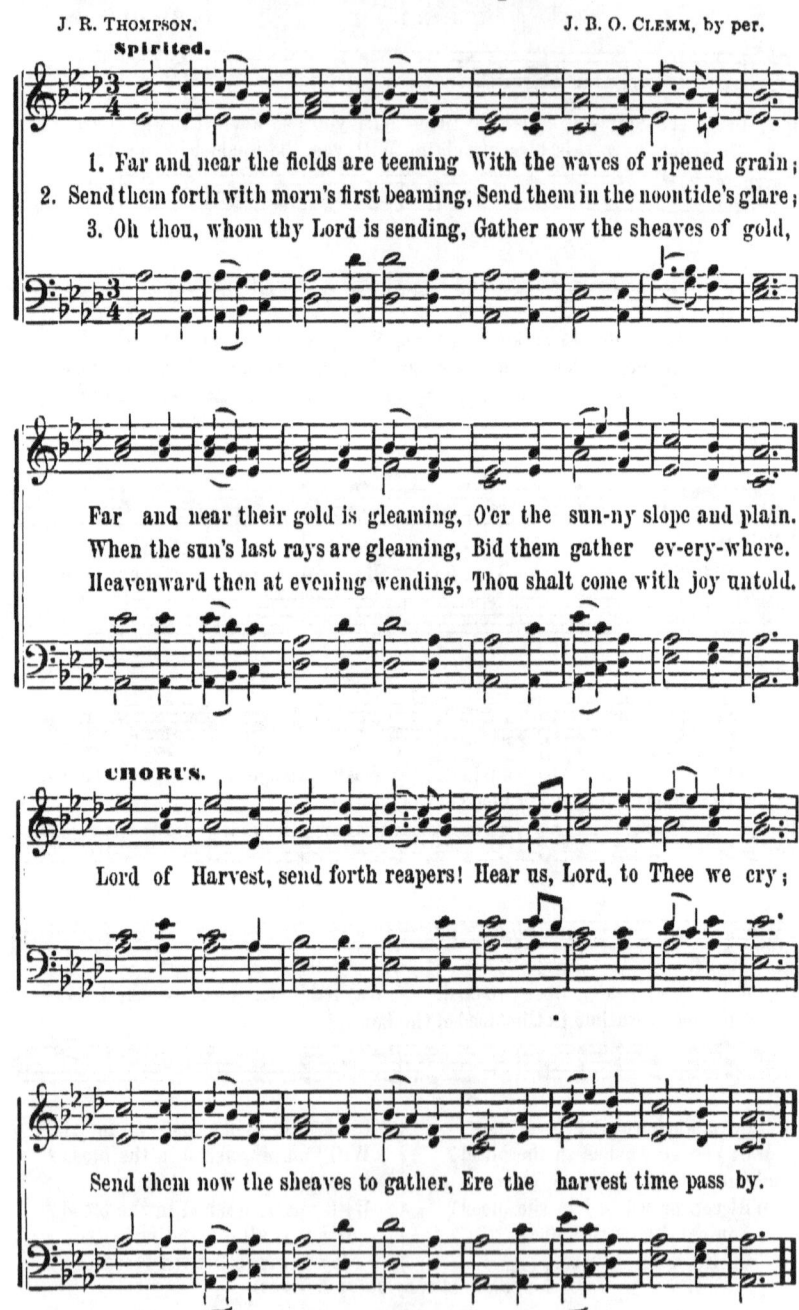

1. Far and near the fields are teeming With the waves of ripened grain;
2. Send them forth with morn's first beaming, Send them in the noontide's glare;
3. Oh thou, whom thy Lord is sending, Gather now the sheaves of gold,

Far and near their gold is gleaming, O'er the sun-ny slope and plain.
When the sun's last rays are gleaming, Bid them gather ev-ery-where.
Heavenward then at evening wending, Thou shalt come with joy untold.

CHORUS.

Lord of Harvest, send forth reapers! Hear us, Lord, to Thee we cry;

Send them now the sheaves to gather, Ere the harvest time pass by.

No. 121. He will Gather the Wheat in His Garner.

HARRIET B. M'KEEVER.   JNO. R. SWENEY, by per.

1. When Jesus shall gather the nations Before Him at last to appear,
2. Shall we hear from the lips of the Savior, The words, Faithful servant, well done;
3. He will smile when He looks on His children, And sees on the ransom'd His seal;

Then, oh, how shall we stand in the judgment, When summoned our sentence to hear?
Or, trembling with fear and with anguish, Be banished away from His throne.
He will clothe them in heavenly beauty, As low at His footstool they kneel.

CHORUS.

He will gather the wheat in His garner, But the chaff will He scatter away;

Then, oh, how shall we stand in the judgment Of the great Resurrection Day?

4 Then let us be watching and waiting,—
Our lamps burning steady and bright,—
When the Bridegroom shall call to the wedding,
Our spirits made ready for flight.

5 Thus living with hearts fixed on heaven,
In patience we wait for the time,
When, the days of our pilgrimage ended,
We'll bask in the presence divine.

No. 122.   Over the Line.

"Let him come unto me."—JOHN 7: 37.

Mrs. K. N. BRADFORD.   EDWARD H. PHELPS, by per.

1. Oh, ten-der and sweet was the Mas-ter's voice As He
2. But my sins are ma-ny, my faith is small, Lo! the
3. But my flesh is weak, I tear-ful-ly said, And the
4. Ah, the world is cold, and I can not go back, Press

lov-ing-ly called to me, "Come o-ver the line, it is
an-swer came quick and clear; "Thou need-est not trust in thy
way I can not see; I fear if I try I may
for-ward I sure-ly must; I will place my hand in His

on-ly a step— I am wait-ing, my child, for thee."
self at all, Step o-ver the line, I am here."
sad-ly fail, And thus may dis-hon-or Thee.
wound-ed palm, Step o-ver the line and trust.

REFRAIN.

"O-ver the line," hear the sweet re-frain, An-gels are

128

Over the Line. Concluded.

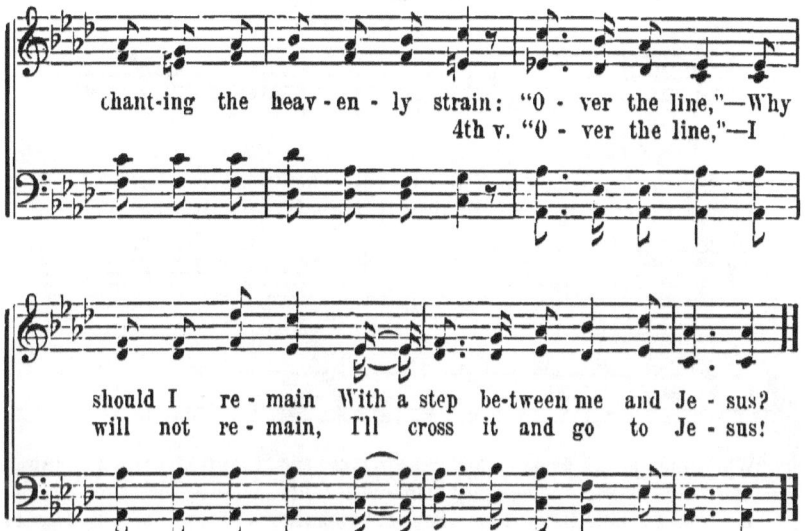

chant-ing the heav-en-ly strain: "O-ver the line,"—Why
should I re-main With a step be-tween me and Je-sus?
4th v. "O-ver the line,"—I
will not re-main, I'll cross it and go to Je-sus!

No. 123. LOWER LIGHTS.
By per.

1 Brightly beams our Father's mercy,
  From his His lighthouse evermore,
  But to us He gives the keeping
  Of the lights along the shore.

  CHORUS.
  Let the lower lights be burning,
  Send a gleam across the wave!
  Some poor struggling, fainting seaman
  You may rescue, you may save.

2 Dark the night of sin has settled,
  Loud the angry billows roar;
  Eager eyes are watching, longing,
  For the lights along the shore.

3 Trim your feeble lamp, my brother!
  Some poor sailor tempest tost,
  Trying now to make the harbor,
  In the darkness may be lost.

P. P. BLISS.

No. 124. JEWELS.
By per.

1 When He cometh, when He cometh,
  To make up His jewels,
  All His jewels, precious jewels,
  His loved and His own.

  CHORUS.
  Like the stars of the morning,
  His bright crown adorning,
  They shall shine in their beauty,
  Bright gems for His crown.

2 He will gather, He will gather,
  The gems for His kingdom;
  All the pure ones all the bright ones,
  His loved and His own.

3 Little children, little children,
  Who love their Redeemer,
  Are the jewels, precious jewels,
  His loved and His own.

Rev. W. O. CUSHING.

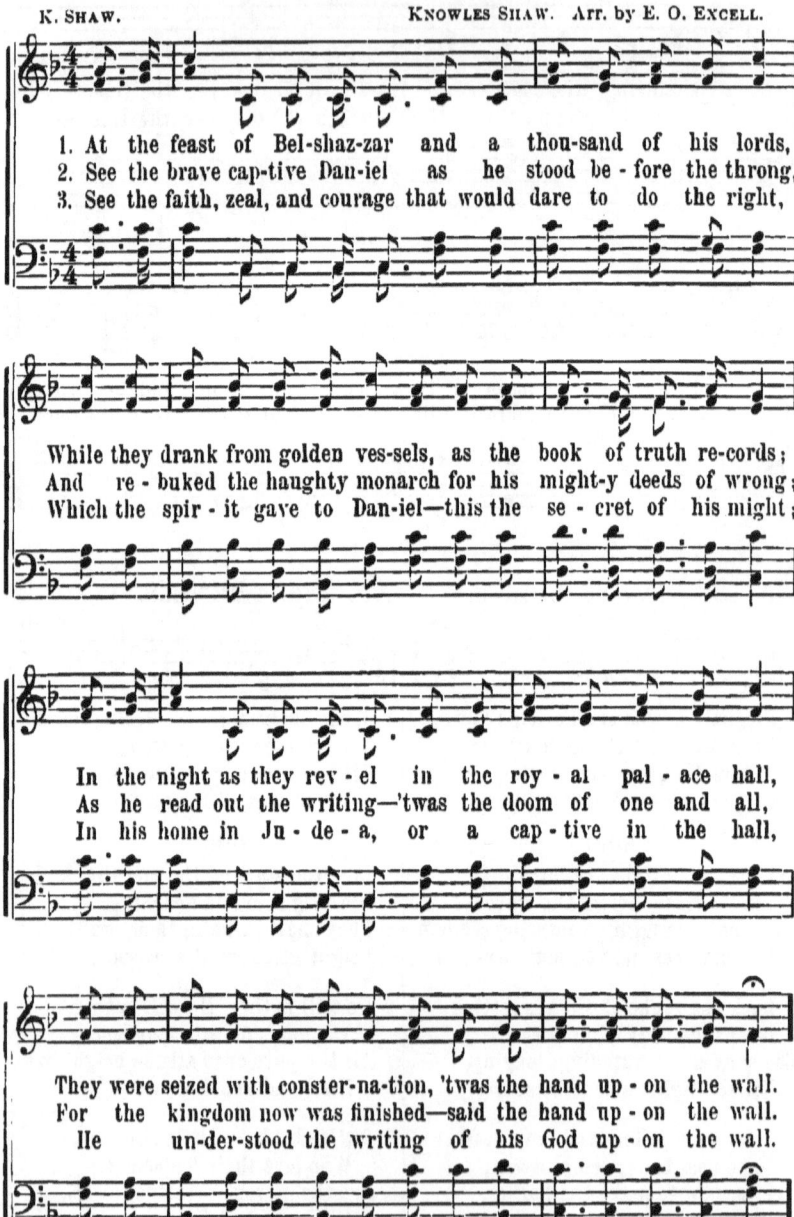

The Handwriting on the Wall. Concluded.

4 So our deeds are recorded—there's a Hand that's writing now,
Sinner, give your heart to Jesus, to His royal mandate bow;
For the day is approaching—it must come to one and all,
When the sinner's condemnation will be written on the wall.

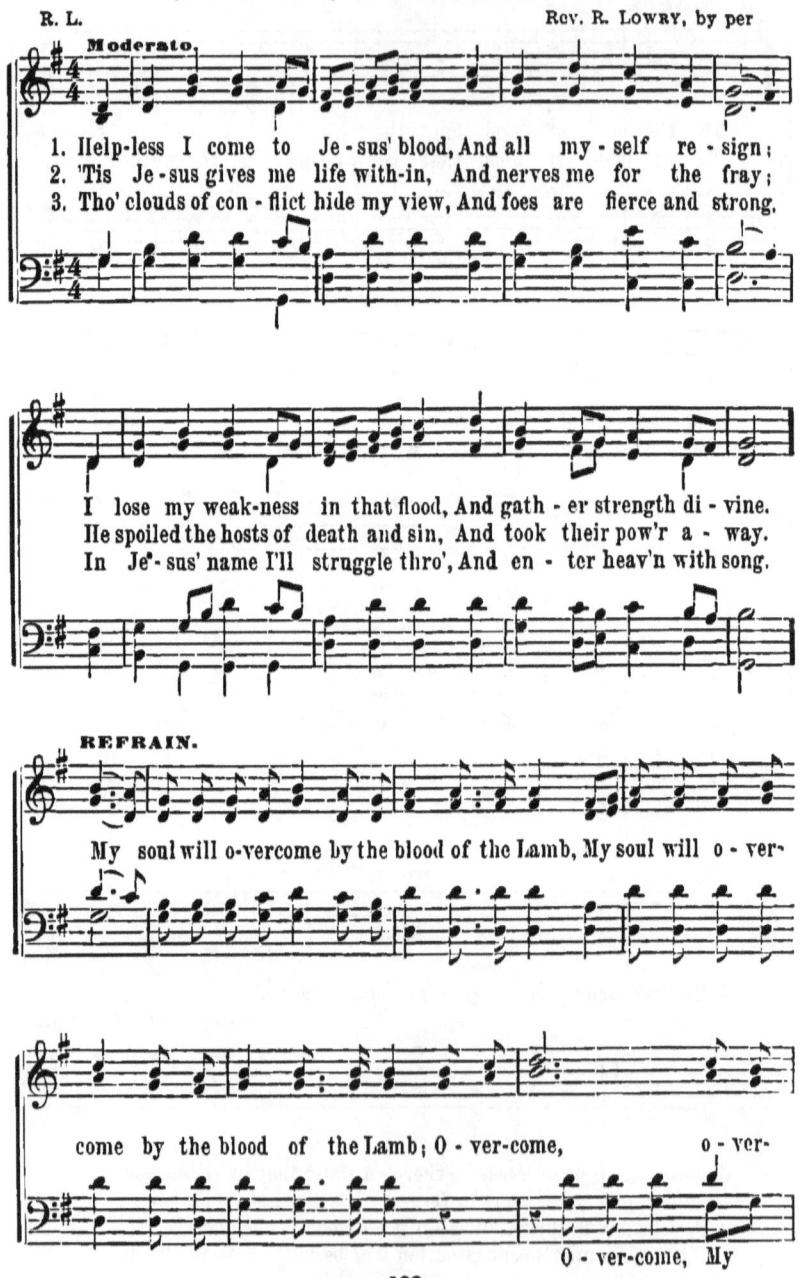

My Soul Will Overcome. Concluded.

come, O-ver-come by the blood of the Lamb.

soul will o-ver-come.

No. 127. RETREAT.

1 From every stormy wind that blows,
From every swelling tide of woes,
There is a calm, a sure retreat,
Tis found beneath the mercy-seat.

2 There is a place where Jesus sheds
The oil of gladness on our heads;
A place than all beside more sweet,
It is the blood-bought mercy-seat.

3 There is a scene where spirits blend,
Where friend holds fellowship with friend:
Though sundered far, by faith they meet
Around one common mercy-seat.
Rev. H. Stowell.

No. 128. ARLINGTON.

1 How precious is the book divine,
By inspiration given;
Bright as a lamp its doctrines shine,
To guide our souls to heaven.

2 It sweetly cheers our drooping hearts,
In this dark vale of tears;
And light, and life, and joy imparts,
To calm our anxious fears.

3 This lamp through all the tedious night
Of life shall guide our way,
Till we behold the clearer light,
Of an eternal day.
Rev. John Fawcett.

No. 129. JESUS LOVES ME.
By per.

1 I am so glad that our Father in heaven (given;
Tells of His love in the book He has
Wonderful things in the Bible I see;
This is the dearest, that Jesus loves me.

REFRAIN—I am so glad, etc.

2. Though I forget Him and wander away,
Still doth He love me wherever I stray;
Back to His dear loving arms would I flee,
When I remember that Jesus loves me.
P. P. Bliss.

No. 130. OLIVET.

1 My faith looks up to Thee,
  Thou Lamb of Calvary,
    Savior divine!
  Now hear me while I pray,
  Take all my guilt away,
  O let me from this day
    Be wholly Thine.

2 May Thy rich grace impart
  Strength to my fainting heart,
    My zeal inspire;
  As Thou hast died for me,
  O may my love to Thee,
  Pure, warm, and changeless be,
    A living fire.
Ray Palmer, D. D.

No. 131. Wonderful Hands of Jesus.

"He lifted up his hands and blessed them."—LUKE 24: 50.

F. G. B.
J. R. MURRAY.

1. O won-derful, won-der-ful hands, So pure, and white, and clean;
2. Such wonderful, wonder-ful hands, So matchless was their grace,
3. Those wonderful, wonder-ful hands, They guard our rugged way;
4. O won-derful, won-der-ful hands, Nail-pierced on Calva-ry!

Tho' midst the vil-est haunts of men Those sacred hands were seen.
They laid a crown and scep-ter down To lift our fall-en race.
They turn the darkest hours of night In-to the brightest day.
Yet, while the blood-drops trickled down, They pled for you and me:

Up-on the head of childhood sweet They left a fond ca-ress;
They touched the poor accursed ones, And made the lep-ers whole;
They heal the mourner's broken heart, They raise each drooping head,
O wounded hands, thy deeds of love For us shall nev-er cease;

The cup of blessings, run-ning o'er, To ag-ed lips would press.
They sent new life thro' palsied limbs, And cleansed the guilty soul.
And e-ven from their si-lent sleep A-wake the pre-cious dead.
Up-lift-ed still their blessings fall And fill our hearts with peace.

Copyright, 1886, by THE JOHN CHURCH CO.

Wonderful Hands of Jesus. Concluded.

Wonder-ful hands, wonder-ful hands Of Christ our Righteous-ness,

Wonder-ful hands, wonder-ful hands Still reaching out to bless.

No. 132. BOYLSTON.

1 A charge to keep I have,
   A God to glorify,
   A never dying soul to save,
   And fit it for the sky.

2 To serve the present age,
   My calling to fulfill,
   O may it all my powers engage,
   To do my Master's will.

3 Arm me with jealous care
   As in Thy sight to live;
   And O, Thy servant, Lord, prepare,
   A strict account to give.

4 Help me to watch and pray.
   And on Thyself rely;
   Assured, if I my trust betray.
   I must forever die.

CHAS. WESLEY.

No. 133. CORONATION.

1 All hail the power of Jesus' name!
   Let angels prostrate fall;
   Bring forth the royal diadem
   And crown Him Lord of all!

2 Sinners, whose love can ne'er forget
   The wormwood and the gall,
   Go spread your trophies at His feet,
   And crown Him Lord of all!

3 Let every kindred, every tribe,
   On this terrestrial ball,
   To Him all majesty ascribe,
   And crown Him Lord of all!

4 O that, with yonder sacred throng,
   We at His feet may fall;
   We'll join the everlasting song,
   And crown Him Lord of all!

Rev. EDWARD PERRONET.

Fall Into Line. Concluded.

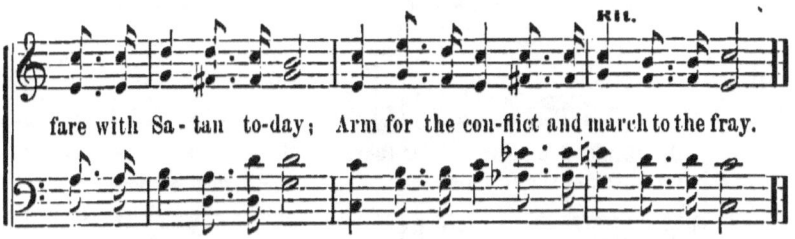

fare with Sa-tan to-day; Arm for the con-flict and march to the fray.

No. 135. THERE IS A FOUNTAIN.

No. 136. NETTLETON.

1 There is a fountain filled with blood,
  Drawn from Immanuel's veins,
And sinners plunged beneath that flood
  Lose all their guilty stains.

REFRAIN.
Lose all their guilty stains,
Lose all their guilty stains,
And sinners plunged beneath that flood
Lose all their guilty stains.

2 The dying thief rejoiced to see
  That fountain in his day;
And there may I, though vile as he,
  Wash all my sins away.

REFRAIN.
Wash all my sins away,
Wash all my sins away,
And there may I, though vile as he,
Wash all my sins away.

3 E'er since by faith I saw the stream
  Thy flowing wounds supply,
Redeeming love has been my theme,
  And shall be till I die.

4 Then in a nobler, sweeter song
  I'll sing thy power to save,
When this poor lisping, stammering
    tongue
  Lies silent in the grave.

1 Come, Thou Fount of every blessing,
  Tune our hearts to sing Thy grace;
Streams of mercy, never ceasing,
  Call for songs of loudest praise.
Teach me some melodious sonnet,
  Sung by flaming tongues above;
Praise the mount, I'm fixed upon it,
  Mount of Thy redeeming love.

2 Here I'll raise my Ebenezer,
  Hither by Thy help I'll come;
And I hope by Thy good pleasure,
  Safely to arrive at home.
Jesus sought me when a stranger,
  Wandering from the fold of God,
He, to rescue me from danger,
  Interposed His precious blood.

3 Oh, to grace how great a debtor,
  Daily I'm constrained to be;
Let Thy goodness, as a fetter,
  Bind my wandering heart to Thee.
Prone to wander, Lord, I feel it,
  Prone to leave the God I love;
Here's my heart, oh take and seal it,
  Seal it for thy courts above.

No. 137. **The Home Over There.**

"O that I had wings like a dove, for then would I fly away and be at rest."— PSALM 55: 6.

Rev. D. W. C. HUNTINGTON. TULLIUS C. O'KANE.

1. Oh, think of a home o-ver there, By the side of the riv-er of light, Where the saints, all immortal and fair, Are robed in their garments of white, o-ver there. O-ver there, o-ver there, o-ver there, Oh, think of a home o-ver there, o-ver there, O-ver there, o-ver there,

2. Oh, think of the friends over there, Who before us the jour-ney have trod, Of the songs that they breathe on the air, In their home in the pal-ace of God, o-ver there. O-ver there, o-ver there, o-ver there, Oh, think of the friends over there, over there, O-ver there, o-ver there,

From "Additional Fresh Leaves," by per.

The Home Over There. Concluded.

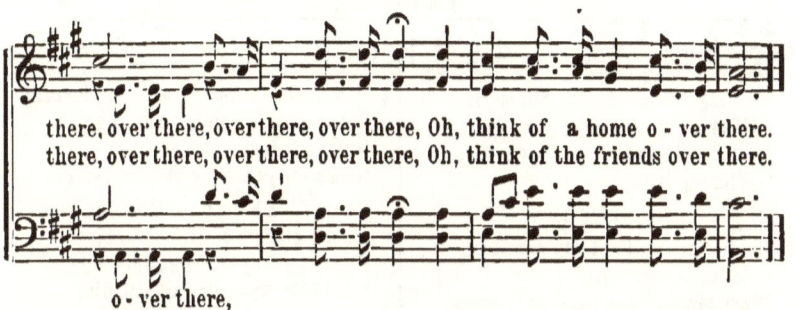

there, over there, over there, over there, Oh, think of a home o-ver there.
there, over there, over there, over there, Oh, think of the friends over there.
o-ver there,

3 My Savior is now over there,
There my kindred and friends are at rest;
Then away from my sorrow and care,
Let me fly to the land of the blest.
Over there, over there,
My Savior is now over there.

4 I'll soon be at home over there,
For the end of my journey I see;
Many dear to my heart, over there,
Are watching and waiting for me.
Over there, over there,
I'll soon be at home over there.

No. 138. BETHANY.

1 Nearer, my God, to Thee,
  Nearer to Thee!
E'en though it be a cross
  That raiseth me,
Still all my song shall be,
Nearer, my God, to Thee,
  Nearer to Thee!

2 Tho' like a wanderer,
  The sun gone down,
Darkness be over me,
  My rest a stone;
Yet in my dreams I'd be
Nearer, my God, to Thee,
  Nearer to Thee!

3 There let my way appear
  Steps unto heaven;
All that Thou sendest me,
  In mercy given;
Angels to beckon me,
Nearer, my God, to Thee,
  Nearer to Thee!
    Mrs. SARAH F. ADAMS.

No. 139. HOUR OF PRAYER.

1 Sweet hour of prayer, sweet hour of prayer,
That calls me from a world of care;
And bids me at my Father's throne,
Make all my wants and wishes known;
In seasons of distress and grief,
My soul has often found relief;
And oft escaped the tempter's snare,
By thy return, sweet hour of prayer,

2 Sweet hour of prayer, sweet hour of prayer,
Thy wings shall my petition bear
To Him, whose truth and faithfulness
Engage the waiting soul to bless;
And since He bids me seek His face,
Believe His word and trust His grace,
I'll cast on Him my every care,
And wait for thee, sweet hour of prayer.
    Rev. W. W. WALFORD.

No. 140. HOLD THE FORT.
By per.

1 Ho! my comrades, see the signal
   Waving in the sky,
Re-inforcements now appearing,
   Victory is nigh.

CHORUS.
Hold the fort, for I am coming,
   Jesus' signal's still;
Wave the answer back to heaven,
   By Thy grace we will.

2 See the mighty host advancing,
   Satan leading on;
Mighty men around us falling,
   Courage almost gone.

3 See the glorious banner waving,
   Hear the bugle blow;
In our Leader's name we'll triumph
   Over every foe.

4 Fierce and long the battle rages,
   But our help is near;
Onward comes our great Commander,
   Cheer, my comrades, cheer!

No. 141. WHAT A FRIEND.

1 Blessed Savior, watch us, guard us,
   As we leave our "Sabbath home."
Guide and keep us from all danger,
   Till again to Thee we come.
Though we very often wander,
   Sorely tempted, prone to sin,
Yet we pray that Thou wouldst hear us,
   Cleanse and make us pure within.

2 Make each spirit meek and lowly,
   Make us leave the ways of strife;
Lead us in the path of duty,
   Lead us to the "better life."
Thus we'd serve Thee, blessed Savior,
   Till we've crossed life's stormy sea;
And with each loved friend and teacher,
   All are gathered home to Thee.

No. 142. PLEYEL'S HYMN.

1 One with Christ! O blessed thought!
   We are by His Spirit taught;
On His fulness now we live,
   Grace for grace we then receive.

2 One with Christ! ye saints rejoice,
   As the objects of His choice;
He will every want supply.
   While He lives we can not die.

3 One with Christ! forever one,
   Debts are paid and work is done;
Grace and glory both are given,
   We are on our way to heaven.
         JOSEPH IRONS.

No. 143. SICILY.

1 Lord, dismiss us with Thy blessing,
   Fill our hearts with joy and peace:
Let us each, Thy love possessing,
   Triumph in redeeming grace;
      Oh, refresh us,
Traveling through this wilderness.

1 Thanks we give, and adoration,
   For Thy gospel's joyful sound;
May the fruits of Thy salvation
   In our hearts and lives abound;
      May Thy presence
With us evermore be found.
         Rev. WALTER SHIRLEY.

No. 144. OLMUTZ.

1 Welcome, sweet day of rest
   That saw the Lord arise;
Welcome to this reviving breast
   And these rejoicing eyes.

2 The King Himself comes near,
   And feasts His saints to-day
Here we may sit, and see Him here,
   And love, and praise, and pray.
         ISAAC WATTS.

No. 145. MISSIONARY HYMN.

1 From Greenland's icy mountains,
From India's coral strand,
Where Afric's sunny fountains
Roll down their golden sand
From many an ancient river,
From many a palmy plain,
They call us to deliver
Their land from error's chain.

2 Shall we whose souls are lighted
With wisdom from on high—
Shall we, to men benighted,
The lamp of life deny?
Salvation—O salvation!
The joyful sound proclaim,
Till earth's remotest nation
Has learned Messiah's name.
BISHOP HEBER.

No. 146. FEDERAL STREET.

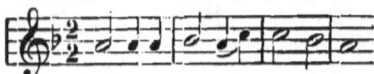

1 They pray the best who pray and watch, (pray,
They watch the best who watch and
They hear Christ's fingers on the latch,
Whether He comes by night, or day.

1 Whether they guard the gates and watch,
Or, patient, toil for Him, and wait,
They hear His fingers on the latch,
If early He doth come, or late.

3 With trembling joy they hail their Lord,
And haste His welcome feet to kiss,
While He, well pleased, doth speak the word
That fills them with unending bliss.
Rev. E. HOPPER.

No. 147. STAND UP FOR JESUS.
Tune, WEBB, No. 64.

1 Stand up! stand up for Jesus!
Ye soldiers of the cross;
Lift high His royal banner,
It must not suffer loss;
From victory unto victory
His army He shall lead,
Till every foe is vanquished,
And Christ is Lord indeed.

2 Stand up! stand up for Jesus!
Stand in His strength alone;
The arm of flesh will fail you—
Ye dare not trust your own,
Put on the gospel armor,
And, watching unto prayer,
Where duty calls, or danger,
Be never wanting there.

3 Stand up! stand up for Jesus!
The strife will not be long!
This day the noise of battle,
The next the victor's song;
To Him that overcometh,
A crown of life shall be;
He with the King of Glory
Shall reign eternally.
Rev. GEO. DUFFIELD, Jr., 1858

No. 148. SWEET HOUR.

1 Obeying Thy divine behest,
We meet, O Christ, to speak of Thee;
Thou art amongst us as a guest,
We feel it, though we can not see;
We seem to breathe, in glad surprise,
An atmosphere of love and bliss,
And read within each other's eyes,
To whom it is we owe all this.

2 How quickly every strife will end,
How soon all idle griefs depart,
When friend takes counsel thus with friend, [meets heart!
When soul meets soul, and heart
We have so many things to say,
So many failings to confess,
Time flies, alas! so soon away,
We can not half we would express.

3 Oh, let us then, dear Lord, be blest,
With Thy sweet presence every day;
Be with us as our daily guest,
And our companion on the way.
Fan our devotion's feeble flame,
Let us press on to things before;
Bring us together in Thy name,
Until we meet to part no more.

No. 149. HENDON.

1 Bless, O Lord, the opening year
To each soul assembled here;
Clothe Thy word with power divine,
Make us willing to be Thine.

2 Where Thou hast Thy work begun,
Give new strength the race to run;
Scatter darkness, doubts and fears,
Wipe away the mourner's tears.

3 Bless us all, both old and young;
Call forth praise from every tongue;
Let the whole assembly prove
All Thy power and all Thy love.
Rev. JOHN NEWTON.

No. 150. DUKE STREET.

1 O Lord, our Guardian and our stay,
Do Thou our humble efforts bless,
And every evil take away,
And spread the cause of righteousness.

2 From day to day Thy power make known,
Thy wisdom and Thy truth divine;
And may we still thy goodness own,
While round our path Thy mercies shine.

3 The drunkard, Lord, in pity see,
A slave to Satan and to sin;
Oh, teach him from all sin to flee;
Restore and make him clean within.

No. 151. WARD.

1 Asleep in Jesus! blessed sleep,
From which none ever wakes to weep,
A calm and undisturbed repose,
Unbroken by the last of foes;

2 Asleep in Jesus! oh, how sweet
To be for such a slumber meet!
With holy confidence to sing
That death has lost its cruel sting.

3 Asleep in Jesus! peaceful rest,
Whose waking is supremely blest;
No fear, no woe shall dim the hour
That manifests the Savior's power.
MARGARET MACKAY.

No. 152. AMERICA.

1 My country 'tis of thee,
Sweet land of liberty,
  Of thee I sing;
Land where my fathers died,
Land of the pilgrim's pride,
From every mountain side
  Let freedom ring.

2 My native country, thee,
Land of the noble free,
  Thy name I love;
I love thy rocks and rills,
Thy woods and templed hills;
My heart with rapture thrills
  Like that above.

3 Our fathers' God! to Thee,
Author of liberty,
  To Thee we sing;
Long may our land be bright
With freedom's holy light;
Protect us by Thy might,
  Great God, our King!
S. F. SMITH, D. D.

No. 153. TEMPERANCE.
Tune—HOLD THE FORT.

1 Brothers! rally for the conflict,
  See the banner wave;
Temperance bands are passing onward,
  Fallen men to save.

CHORUS.

Hear a mighty host of freemen
  Songs of triumph raise;
Love hath conquered, chains are broken,
  Give to God the praise.

2 Burst the tyrant's bands asunder,
  Set the captives free;
Let rejoicing wives and mothers
  Shout the jubilee.—Cho.
WM. STEVENSON.

No. 154. What Shall the Harvest be?

"Whatsoever a man soweth, that shall he also reap."—GAL. 6: 7.

Mrs. EMILY S. OAKEY, 1850. *Alt.*   P. P. BLISS, by per.

1. Sowing the seed by the daylight fair, Sowing the seed by the noontide glare,
2. Sowing the seed by the wayside high, Sowing the seed on the rocks to die,
3. Sowing the seed of a lingering pain, Sowing the seed of a maddened brain,
4. Sowing the seed with an aching heart, Sowing the seed while the tear-drops start,

Sowing the seed by the fading light, Sowing the seed in the solemn night;
Sowing the seed where the thorns will spoil, Sowing the seed in the fertile soil;
Sowing the seed of a tarnished name, Sowing the seed of e-ter-nal shame;
Sowing in hope till the reapers come, Gladly to gather the harvest home;

Oh, what shall the harvest be? . . . . Oh, what shall the harvest be?

What Shall the Harvest be? Concluded.

No. 155. A Sinner like Me.

C. J. B.
C. J. BUTLER by per.

1. I was once far away from the Sav-ior, And as vile as a sin-ner could be, I won-dered if Christ the Re-deem-er, Could save a poor sin-ner like me.
2. I wan-dered on in the dark-ness, Not a ray of light could I see, And the thought filled my heart with sad-ness, There's no hope for a sin-ner like me.
3. And then, in that dark lone-ly hour, A voice whispered sweetly to me, Say-ing, Christ the Re-deem-er has power, To save a poor sin-ner like me.

4 I listened, and lo! 'twas the Savior
That was speaking so kindly to me;
I cried, I'm the chief of sinners,
Thou canst save a poor sinner like me.

5 I then fully trusted in Jesus,
And oh! what a joy came to me;
My heart was filled with His praises,
For saving a sinner like me.

6 No longer in darkness I'm walking,
For the light is now shining on me,
And now unto others I'm telling
How He saved a poor sinner like me.

7 And when life's journey is over,
And I the dear Savior shall see,
I'll praise Him forever and ever,
For saving a sinner like me.

Copyright, 1881, by JOHN J. HOOD.

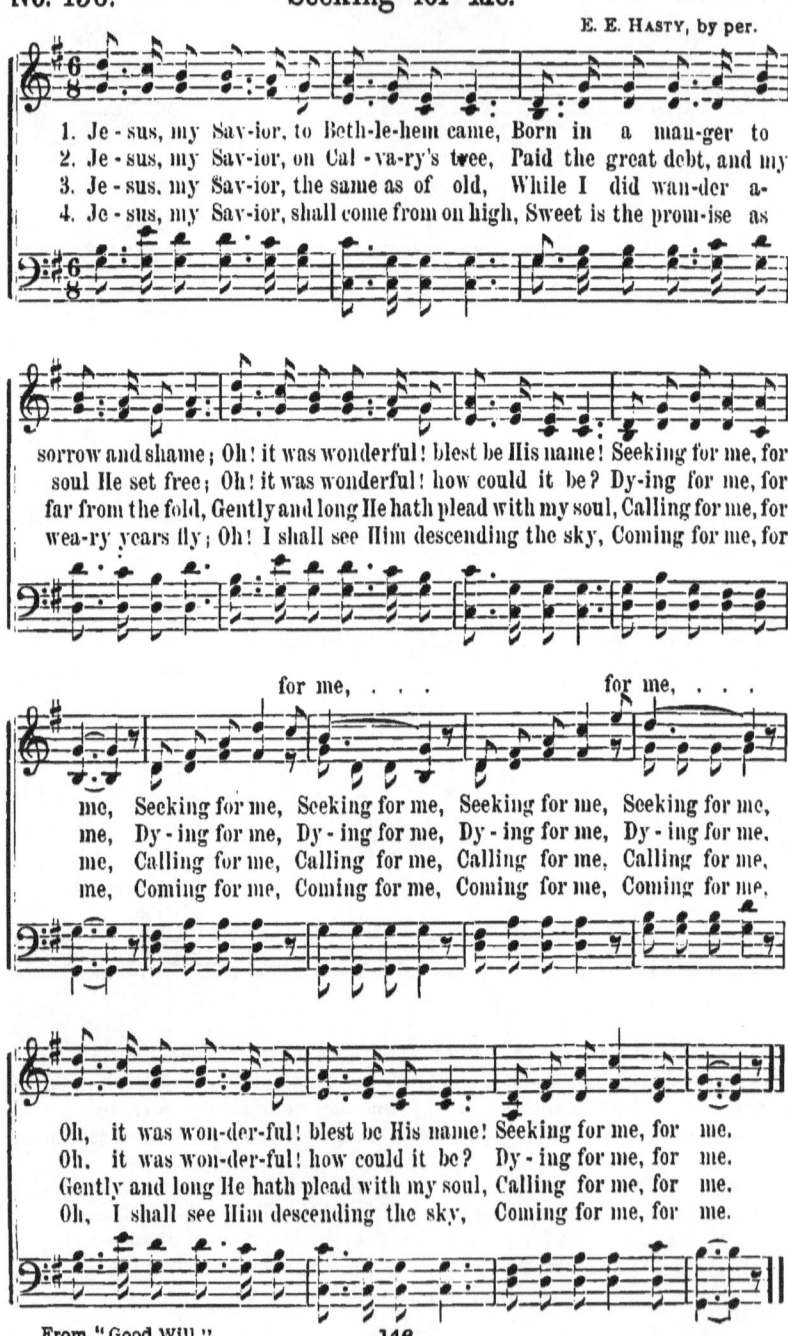

No. 157. Ring the Bells of Heaven.

"There is joy in the presence of the angels of God over one sinner that repenteth."--LUKE 15: 10.

REV. WM. O. CUSHING.   GEO. F. ROOT, by per.

Joyfully.

1. Ring the bells of heav - en! there is joy to-day, For a soul re-turning from the wild; See! the Father meets him out upon the way, Wel-com-ing his weary, wand'ring child.
2. Ring the bells of heav - en! there is joy to-day, For the wand'rer now is re - con - ciled; Yes, a soul is rescued from his sin-ful way, And is born a - new, a ransomed child.
3. Ring the bells of heav - en! spread the feast to-day, Angels, swell the glad triumphant strain! Tell the joy-ful tidings, bear it far a - way! For a precious soul is born a - gain.

CHORUS.

Glo - ry! glo - ry! how the an-gels sing; Glo-ry! glory! how the loud harps ring; 'Tis the ransomed ar - my, like a mighty sea, Pealing forth the anthem of the free.

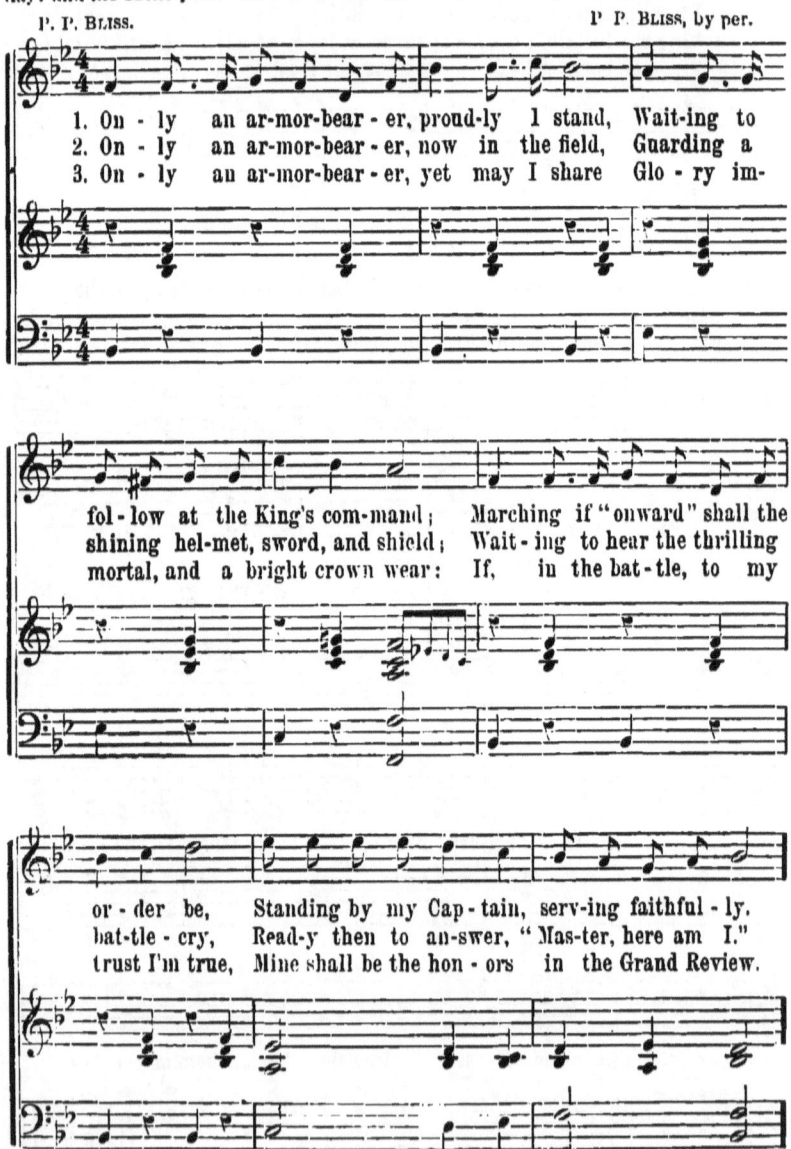

Only an Armor-Bearer. Concluded.

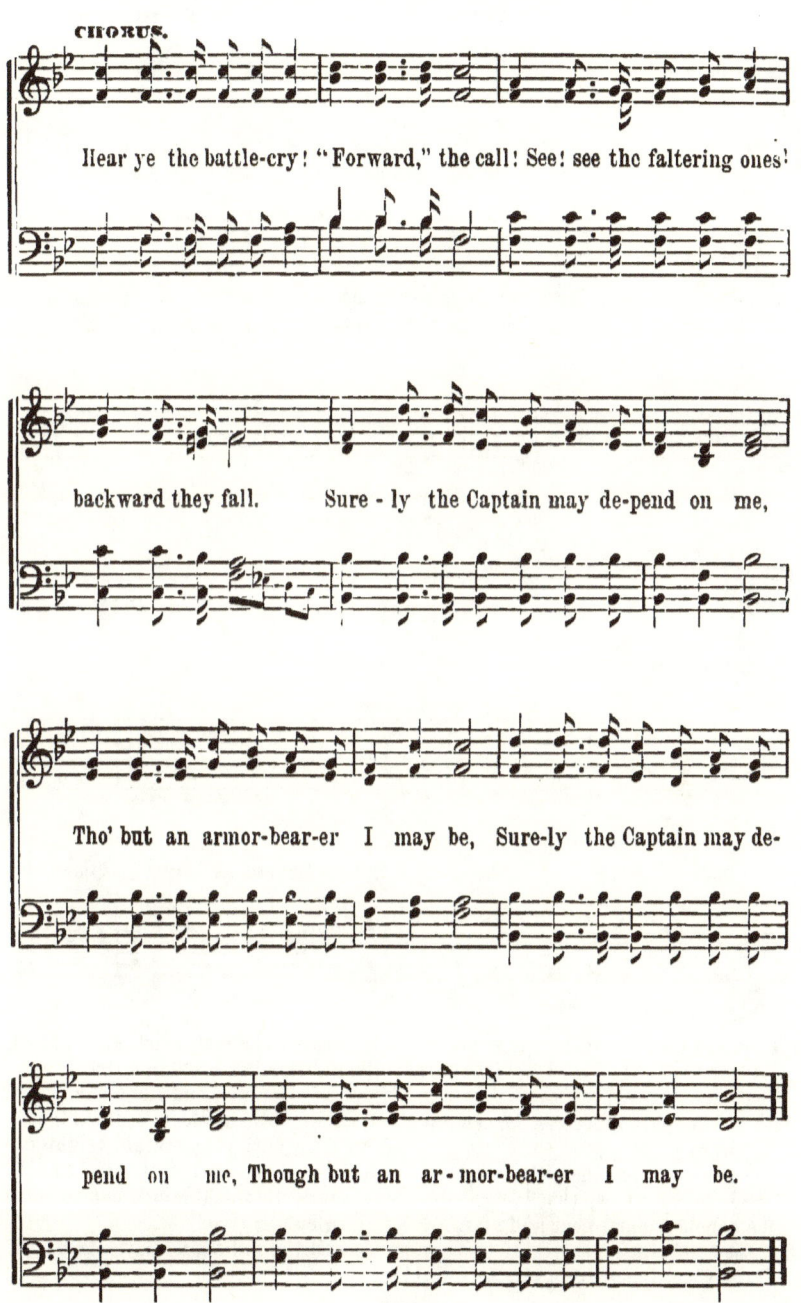

No. 159. Say, is Your Lamp Burning?

(To W. B. Jacobs.) E. O. Excell, by per.

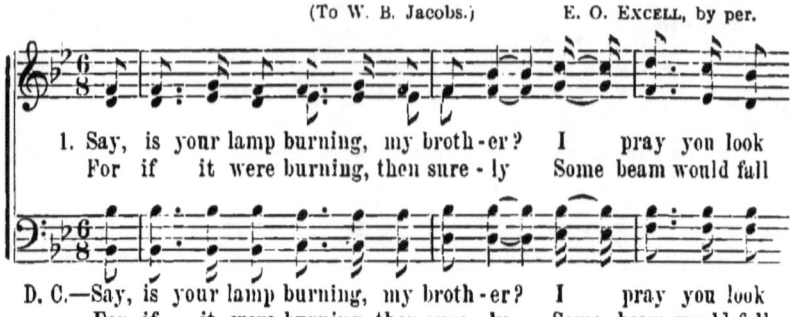

1. Say, is your lamp burning, my broth-er? I pray you look
For if it were burning, then sure-ly Some beam would fall

D. C.—Say, is your lamp burning, my broth-er? I pray you look
For if it were burning, then sure-ly Some beam would fall

quick-ly and see, ⎱ ⎰ There are ma-ny and ma-ny a-
bright-ly on me. ⎱ ⎰ If you thought that they walked in the

quick-ly and see. ⎱
bright-ly on me. ⎰

round you, Who follow wherever you go.
shad-ow, Your . . . . , lamp would burn brighter, I know.

2 Upon the dark mountians they stum-
ble, [they lie
They are bruised on the rocks and
With white pleading faces turned up-
ward
To the clouds and the pitiful sky;
There is many a lamp that is lighted,
We behold them a-near and afar,
But not many among them, my brother,
Shine steadily on like a star.—D. C.

3 If once all the lamps that are lighted
Should steadily blaze in a line
Wide over the land and the ocean,
What a girdle of glory would shine!
How all the dark places would brighten,
How the mists would roll up and away!
How the earth would laugh out in her
gladness
To hail the millenniel day.—D. C.

No. 160. Yield Not to Temptation.

"God is faithful, who will not suffer you to be tempted above that ye are able."—1 COR. 10: 13.

H. R. PALMER.   H. R. PALMER, by per.

1. Yield not to temp-ta-tion, For yielding is sin, Each vic-t'ry will help you Some oth-er to win; Fight manful-ly on-ward, Dark passions subdue, Look e-ver to Je-sus, He'll carry you through.

2. Shun e-vil com-pan-ions, Bad language dis-dain, God's name hold in rev'rence, Nor take it in vain; Be thoughtful and earn-est, Kind-hearted and true, Look e-ver to Je-sus, He'll carry you through.

3. To him that o'ercometh God giveth a crown, Thro' faith we shall con-quer, Though often cast down; He who is our Sav-ior, Our strength will renew, Look ever to Je-sus, He'll carry you through.

CHORUS.

Ask the Sav-ior to help you, Comfort, strengthen and keep you; He is will-ing to aid you, He will car-ry you through.

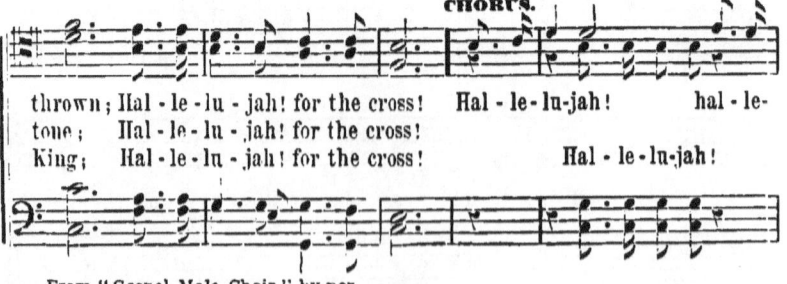

Hallelujah For the Cross. Concluded.

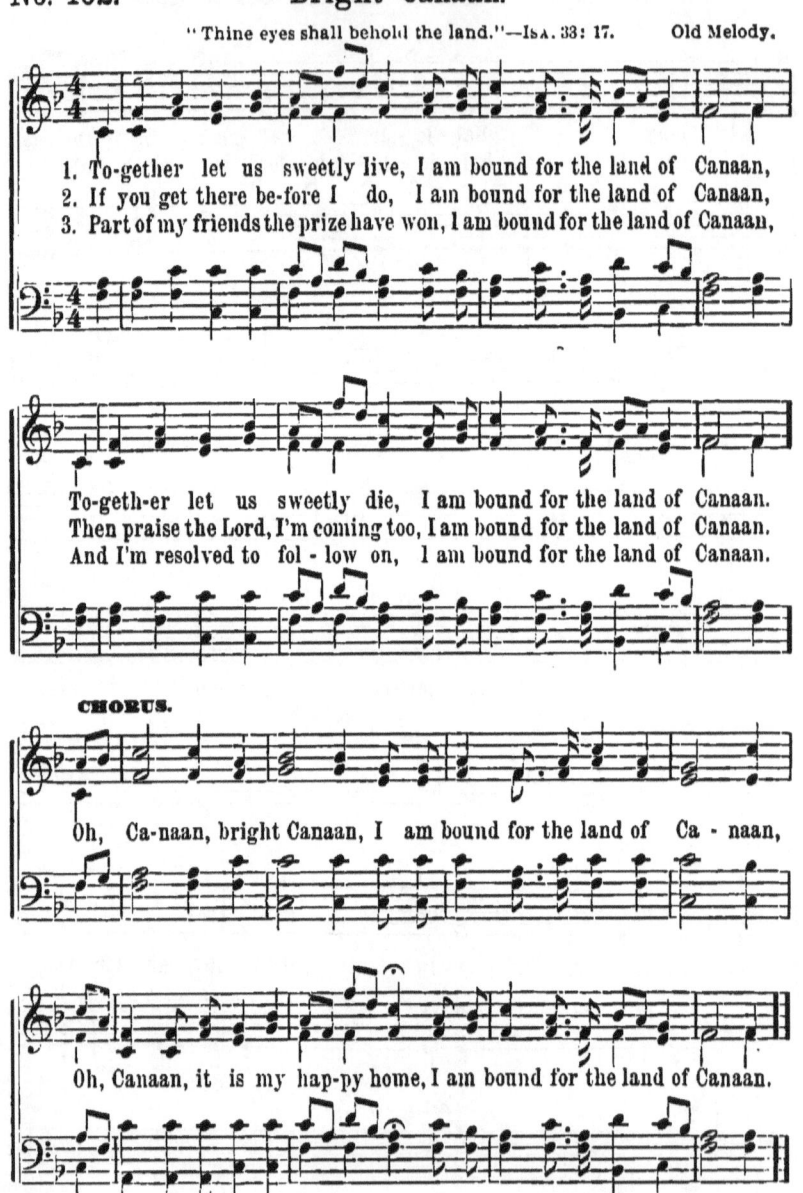

No. 162. Bright Canaan.

"Thine eyes shall behold the land."—Isa. 33: 17.   Old Melody.

1. To-gether let us sweetly live, I am bound for the land of Canaan,
2. If you get there be-fore I do, I am bound for the land of Canaan,
3. Part of my friends the prize have won, I am bound for the land of Canaan,

To-geth-er let us sweetly die, I am bound for the land of Canaan.
Then praise the Lord, I'm coming too, I am bound for the land of Canaan.
And I'm resolved to fol-low on, I am bound for the land of Canaan.

CHORUS.

Oh, Ca-naan, bright Canaan, I am bound for the land of Ca-naan,

Oh, Canaan, it is my hap-py home, I am bound for the land of Canaan.

4 Then come with me, beloved friend,
   I am bound for the land of Canaan,
The joys of heaven shall never end,
   I am bound for the land of Canaan.

5 Our songs of praise shall fill the skies,
   I am bound for the land of Canaan,
While higher still our joys they rise,
   I am bound for the land of Canaan.

No. 163. Old Hundred. L. M.

Or the following tune may be used.

No. 164. Sessions. L. M.

L. O. Emerson.

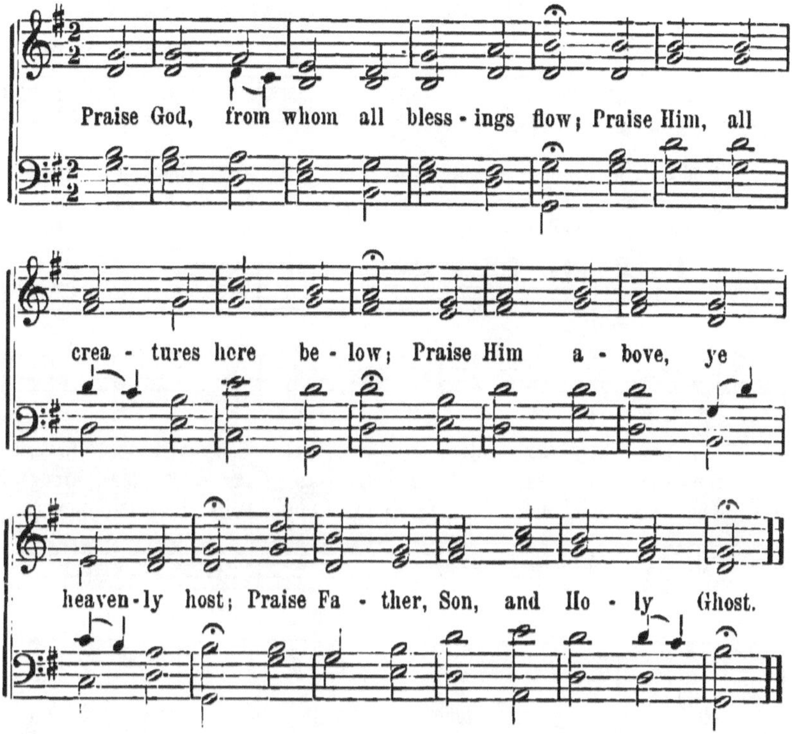

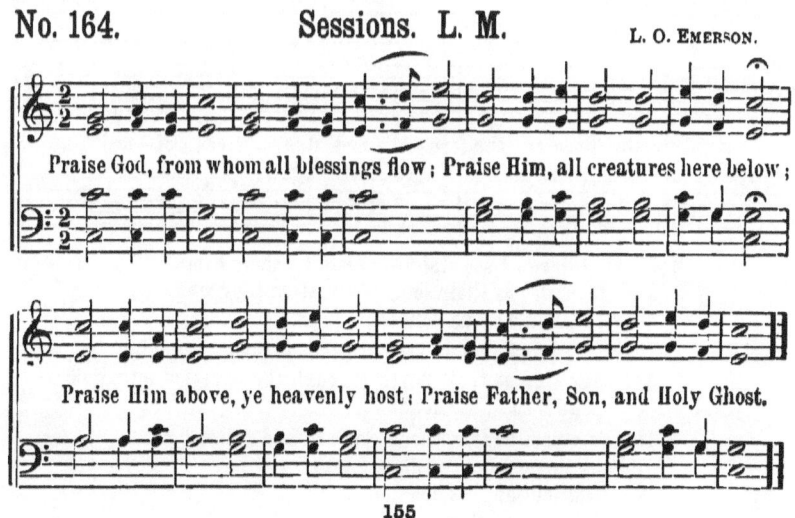

No. 165. Hallelujah, 'tis Done.

"For God so loved the world, that he gave his only begotten Son, that whosoever believeth in him, should not perish, but have everlasting life."—JOHN 3: 16.

P. P. BLISS. P. P. BLISS, by per.

1. 'Tis the prom-ise of God, full sal-va-tion to give
2. Tho' the path-way be lone-ly, and dan-ger-ous too,
3. Ma-ny loved ones have I in yon heav-en-ly throng,

Un-to him who on Je-sus, his Son, will be-lieve.
Sure-ly Je-sus is a-ble to car-ry me through.
They are safe now in glo-ry, and this is their song:

Hal-le-lu-jah, 'tis done! I be-lieve on the Son; I am saved by the blood of the cru-ci-fied One; cru-ci-fied One.

4 Little children I see standing close by their King,
And He smiles as their song of salvation they sing
Hallelujah, 'tis done! etc.

5 There are prophets and kings in that throng I behold,
And they sing as they march through the streets of pure gold:
Hallelujah, 'tis done! etc.

6 There's a part in that chorus for you and for me,
And the theme of our praises forever will be:
Hallelujah, 'tis done! etc.

No. 166. Opening Service.

By W. B. JACOBS

Supt.—For God so loved the world, that he gave his only begotten Son, that whosoever believeth in Him should not perish, but have everlasting life.—JOHN 3: 16.

Sch.—In this was manifested the love of God toward us, because that God sent His only begotten Son into the world, that we might live through Him.—JOHN 4: 9.

Supt.—Beloved, if God so loved us, we ought also to love one another.—JOHN 4: 11.

REVIVE US AGAIN.

1 We praise Thee, oh, God! for the Son
 of Thy love, [above.
For Jesus who died, and is now gone
CHO.—Hallelujah! Thine the glory,
 Hallelujah! Amen!
Hallelujah! Thine the glory,
 Revive us again.

Supt.—But the Comforter, which is the Holy Ghost, whom the Father will send in my name, He shall teach you all things, and bring all things to your remembrance, whatsoever I have said unto you.—JOHN 14: 26.

Sch.—When He, the Spirit of truth, is come, He will guide you into all truth: for He shall not speak of Himself; but whatsoever He shall hear, that shall He speak: and He will show you things to come.—JOHN 16: 13.

Supt.—He shall glorify me: for He shall receive of mine, and shall show it unto you.—JOHN 16: 14.

REVIVE US AGAIN.

2 We praise Thee, O God! for Thy Spirit
 of light, [scattered our night.
Who has shown us our Savior and
CHO.—Hallelujah! etc.

Supt.—And I beheld, and I heard the voice of many angels round about the throne, and the living creatures and the elders; and the number of them was ten thousand times ten thousand, and thousands of thousands.—REV. 5: 11.

Sch.—Saying with a loud voice. Worthy is the Lamb that was slain to receive power and riches, and wisdom and strength, and honor, and, glory, and blessing.—REV. 5: 12.

REVIVE US AGAIN.

3 All glory and praise to the Lamb that
 was slain, [cleansed every stain.
Who has borne all our sins, and has
CHO.—Hallelujah! etc.

Copyright, 1885, by E. O. EXCELL.

CONTENTS.

Titles in Caps; First Lines in Roman.

	No.		No.
A charge to keep I have	132	DRAW ME NEARER	27
A SINNER LIKE ME	155	DRIFTING AWAY FROM JESUS	30
ALMOST	74	DUKE ST. L. M.	150
ALMOST PERSUADED	22	DARE TO BE A DANIEL	103
All hail the power of Jesus' name	133	ETERNITY IS DRAWING NIGH	66
AMERICA	152	EVER WILL I PRAY	79
Amazing grace how sweet	68	FALL INTO LINE	134
ARISE, WORK, AND PRAY	111	Father, in the morning	79
ARLINGTON	128	Far and near the fields	120
ARE YOU READY	13	FEDERAL ST. L. M.	146
Are you ready for the bridegroom	116	From every stormy wind	127
Are you clinging	56	From Greenland's icy mountains	145
ARE YOU WASHED IN THE BLOOD	11	GATHER THEM IN	41
Are you trusting in the Savior	118	GLORIOUS FOUNTAIN	24
Are you weary	76	GLORY TO HIS NAME	115
Arise, my soul, arise	43	GLORIA PATRI	32
Asleep in Jesus	151	Glory be to the Father	32
At the feast of Belshazzar	125	GO FORTH TO THE FIELD	101
BEULAH LAND	69	GOD BE WITH YOU	38
BEAUTIFUL LAND ON HIGH	10	HALLELUJAH, 'TIS DONE	165
BETHANY	138	HALLELUJAH FOR THE CROSS	161
BEHOLD THE BRIDEGROOM	116	Have you been to Jesus	11
Blest be the tie that binds	20	Have you on the Lord believed	42
Blessed Savior, watch us	141	HAPPY DAY	1
Bless, O Lord, the opening year	149	HEAR THE CALL	23
BOYLSTON. S. M.	132	Hear the Savior sweetly saying	3
BRIGHT CANAAN	162	Hear ye the glad, good news	80
Brightly beams our Father's mercy	123	HE THAT BELIEVETH	80
BRINGING IN THE SHEAVES	67	HE WILL GATHER THE WHEAT	121
Brothers, rally for the conflict	153	HENDON. 7s	149
CALL THEM IN	3	Helpless I come to Jesus' blood	126
CALVARY	86	HIDING, DEAR LORD, IN THEE	8
Called to the feast	52	Ho! my comrades	140
CHRIST ALONE	72	HOLD THE FORT	140
CLINGING CLOSE TO JESUS	56	Holy Bible, book divine	50
CLOSE TO THEE	46	HOUR OF PRAYER	139
CORONATION	133	How precious is the book divine	128
Come thou Fount of	136	I am thine, O Lord	27
COMPANIONSHIP WITH JESUS	61	I am so glad that our Father	129
Come every soul by sin oppressed	60	I COULD NOT DO WITHOUT THEE	58
Come we that love the Lord	63	I gave my life for thee	6
CROSS AND CROWN	87	I have a song I love to sing	12
CHRIST RECEIVETH SINFUL MEN	90	I hear a sweet voice	4
DENNIS. S. M.	20	I have found repose	31
Down at the cross	115	I once was far away	155
Down life's dark vale	17	I WILL LET HIM IN	81

(158)

INDEX.

Title	No.
I will sing of my Redeemer	19
I Want to be a Worker	45
Is There Oil in your Lamp	35
Is my Name written There	77
It is Well with my Soul	75
I've a guide, tho' the way	88
I've reached the land of	69
I've found a friend in Jesus	53
I've Washed my Robes	73
It is Good to be Here	54
Jesus knocks at the door of	81
Jewels	124
Jesus Loves Me	129
Jesus is Calling	93
Jesus is tenderly calling thee	93
Jesus is pleading with my poor soul	7
Jesus, my Lord, to thee I cry	78
Jesus, my Savior	156
Jesus will Give you Rest	117
Jesus will Help You	104
Just for To-day	70
Just as I am	109
Leaning on Jesus	92
Let us gather up the sunbeams	108
Let us sing redemption's story	16
Lenox. H. M	43
Let Him In	82
Let the Master in	113
Light in the darkness, sailor	48
Like a bird on the deep	14
List, the spirit calls to thee	119
Lower Lights	123
Lord, for to-morrow and its needs	70
Lord, dismiss us with thy	143
Lord, I care not for riches	77
Lo, the day of God is breaking	23
My Redeemer	19
More to Follow	42
My Prayer	59
More holiness give me	59
My hope is built on nothing less	83
Must Jesus bear the cross alone	87
My Father is rich in houses and lands	99
My robes were once all stained	73
My Soul will Overcome	126
My faith looks up to thee	130
Missionary Hymn	145
My country, 'tis of thee	152
Marcellus. 7s	50
My soul rejoicing fain would raise	91
Meet Me There	102
Nettleton	136
Nearer, my God, to thee	138
Obeying thy divine behest	148
O'er the dreary mountains	65
O'er Jordan's dark and stormy	57
O happy day that fixed my choice	1
Oh, blessed fellowship divine	61
Oh, Crown of Rejoicing	51
O Lord, our guardian and our stay	150
Old Hundred. L. M	163
Olivet	130
Olmutz. S. M	144
Once I heard a sound	113
Only Trust Him	60
Only an Armor-bearer	158
On Calvary's brow	86
One with Christ	142
Oh, tender and sweet was the	122
Oh, 'tis Glory in My Soul	28
Oh, when shall I sweep thro' the	33
Oh, sorrowing mortal	21
Oh, think of the home over there	137
Oh, let the story oft be told	47
O Prodigal, do'nt Stay Away	49
Our Glad Jubilee	36
Over the Line	122
Over the Threshold	84
O wonderful, wonderful hands	131
On the happy golden shore	102
Praise God from whom	164
Pray, brethren, pray	66
Precious Promise	15
Pull for the Shore	48
Pleyel's Hymn	142
Redemption's Story	16
Rescue the Perishing	40
Repeat the story o'er and o'er	89
Retreat	127
Rejoicing Evermore	62
Redeeming Love	91
Revive us Again	166
Ring the Bells of Heaven	157
Say, is Your Lamp Burning	159
Scatter Seeds of Kindness	108
Seeking to Save	71
Seeking for Me	156
Sessions. L. M	164
Shall I be Saved To-night	7
Should the summons, quickly	13
Sicily. 8s & 7s	143
Since I Have Been Redeemed	12
Sing them over again to me	9
Sinners, Jesus will receive	90
Somewhere, says a mother	111
So will I Comfort you	21
So near the door	74
Sound the Battle Cry	39
Sowing in the morning	67
Sowing the seed by the daylight	154
Stand up for Jesus	147
Step over the threshold	84

INDEX.

	No.		No.
Sweet hour of prayer.	139	Trusting in the Promise.	31
Sweet Rest at Home.	57	Trusting Jesus.	118
Standing by a purpose true.	103	Trusting in the Lord.	25
Simply trusting every day.	112	The Lily of the Valley.	53
Take me as I am.	78	The Savior is calling you, sinner.	104
Tenderly the Shepherd.	71	Trusting Jesus that is All.	112
Tell it to Jesus alone.	76	Warwick. C. M.	68
Temperance.	150–153	Ward. L. M.	151
That which was Lost.	65	Wake, wake the song.	36
That Old, Old Story is True.	37	We will Pray for one Another.	34
The Crown.	98	Webb.	64
The Child of a King.	99	Welcome, sweet day of rest.	144
The Crown of Glory.	4	Welcome for Me.	14
The cross, it standeth.	161	Welcome to Glory.	33
The Call for Reapers.	120	Weary with watching alone.	92
The Great Physician.	97	We shall stand before the King.	85
The Home over There.	137	We praise thee, O God.	166
The Half was Never Told.	89	We're going Home To-morrow.	29
The Handwriting on the Wall.	125	We're Marching to Zion.	63
The Light of the World is Jesus.	5	When Jesus Comes.	17
The Mistakes of My Life.	110	When Jesus shall gather.	121
The morning light is breaking.	64	When the King comes In.	52
The Ninety and Nine.	55	When peace like a river.	75
The Pathway of Life.	88	When he cometh.	124
The Pure Water of Life.	100	When Jesus Walked in Galilee.	47
The Solid Rock.	83	What a Friend.	141
The Sure Foundation.	18	What a friend we have in Jesus.	96
The whole world was lost.	5	What hast thou done for me.	6
There stands a Rock.	18	What Shall the Harvest be.	154
There's a crown of gold.	98	Where is my Boy To-night.	100
There s a beautiful river.	100	Whosoever Will.	2
There's Much we Can do.	44	Whosoever heareth.	2
There's stranger at the door.	82	Who Cares for a Soul.	26
There's a wonderful story.	37	Who'll be the Next.	95
There's a beautiful land on high.	10	Wonderful Words of Life.	9
There is a fountain.	24–135	Wonderful Hands of Jesus.	131
There were ninety and nine.	55	Why do you Wait.	94
They pray the best.	146	While we bow in thy name.	54
'Tis the promise of God.	165	What a Meeting that will Be.	105
Tho' the storms of life.	25	When we all meet at home.	105
Tho' troubles assail.	62	Who's on the Lord's side.	114
Thou Hast Called Me.	107	We're marching to Canaan.	114
Thou my everlasting portion.	46	Will you be Washed in the.	119
Together let us sweetly.	162	Yield not to Temptation.	160
To thy cross, dear Christ.	28		

www.ingramcontent.com/pod-product-compliance
Lightning Source LLC
Chambersburg PA
CBHW030256170426

43202CB00009B/761